It's Not What You Teach But How

How do we prepare students to become problem-finders, innovators, and entrepreneurs who can thrive in a global society? The Common Core charts a pathway to success, yet we know that checking off each standard one by one will not achieve the kind of results we want. This powerful book by bestselling author Nancy Sulla has the answers. She explains how teachers can bring students to deeper levels of learning by shifting from the *what* to the *how* of the CCSS. She offers seven insights that you can use to teach the standards in a more meaningful way, to bring all of your students to true understanding and application.

You'll uncover how to:

♦ **Incorporate ends-based teaching** to ensure that the instructional focus is on the ultimate goal of each standard and not just on the basic skills;

♦ **Encourage grappling with content** through structured techniques such as problem-based learning, questioning, and simulations;

♦ **Use cognitive progression,** by understanding how the brain learns, to produce real results;

♦ **Harness the power of language** in all disciplines, not just in English language arts;

♦ **Build executive function** in the brain rather than focusing on academic function alone;

♦ **Increase retention** by using learning and practice activities in different ways and by differentiating instruction; and

♦ **Become a true facilitator**, not just a responder to students' questions.

Throughout the book, you'll find a variety of practical examples from across the curriculum, as well as "Your Turn" opportunities to help you try the ideas in your own classroom.

The future may not be easily defined, but it can be shaped by teachers who are right now preparing the next generation of world citizens.

Nancy Sulla is the founder and President of IDE Corp. (Innovative Designs for Education), a consulting company specializing in instructional and organizational design. She is also the author of *Students Taking Charge: Inside the Learner-Active, Technology-Infused Classroom* (Routledge, 2011).

Other Eye On Education Books Available From Routledge

(www.routledge.com/eyeoneducation)

Students Taking Charge: Inside the Learner-Active, Technology-Infused Classroom
Nancy Sulla

Inquiry and Innovation in the Classroom: Using 20% Time, Genius Hour, and PBL to Drive Student Success
A. J. Juliani

Reinventing Writing: The 9 Tools That Are Changing Writing, Teaching, and Learning Forever
Vicki Davis

Engaged, Connected, Empowered
Ben Curran and Neil Wetherbee

Rigor is NOT a Four-Letter Word
Barbara R. Blackburn

Rigor in Your Classroom: A Toolkit for Teachers
Barbara R. Blackburn

Seven Simple Secrets: What the BEST Teachers Know and Do!, 2nd Edition
Annette Breaux and Todd Whitaker

101 Answers for New Teachers and Their Mentors: Effective Teaching Tips for Daily Classroom Use, 2nd Edition
Annette Breaux

What Teachers Can Learn From Sports Coaches: A Playbook of Instructional Strategies
Nathan Barber

It's Not What You Teach But How

7 Insights to Making the CCSS Work for You

Nancy Sulla

Routledge
Taylor & Francis Group

NEW YORK AND LONDON

First published 2015
by Routledge
711 Third Avenue, New York, NY 10017

and by Routledge
2 Park Square, Milton Park, Abingdon, Oxon, OX14 4RN

Routledge is an imprint of the Taylor & Francis Group, an informa business

Library of Congress Cataloging-in-Publication Data
Sulla, Nancy.
   It's not what you teach but how : 7 insights to making the CCSS work for you / by Nancy Sulla.
      pages cm
   Includes bibliographical references.
   1. Education—Standards—United States.   2. Common Core State Standards (Education)
   3. Critical thinking—Study and teaching.   I. Title.
CURIL LB3060.83.S87 2015
      370.973—dc23
      2014044539

ISBN: 978-0-415-73477-6 (hbk)
ISBN: 978-0-415-73340-3 (pbk)
ISBN: 978-1-315-81973-0 (ebk)

Typeset in Palatino LT Std
by Apex CoVantage, LLC

To Mom and Dad

Contents

Acknowledgments

I would like to thank Fiona Borland: You inspired me to tackle the melding of the CCSS with the *Learner-Active, Technology-Infused Classroom* and generously contributed your thoughts and words to the process.

Thanks to Lauren Davis, my editor at Routledge: You supported me tremendously with your feedback, ideas, and endless patience.

I am incredibly blessed to work with a group of colleagues who are dedicated to making a difference in the world of education. I so appreciate your insights; ideas; stories; feedback on the manuscript; support; and the high-quality, collaborative culture you have created at IDE Corp. So thank you to Boyd Adolfsson, Tanya Bosco, Chris Freisen, Brian Giddens, Lynn Gorey, Dan Gross, Felicia Hillman, Nicole Koch, Sharon Kubart, Millie Matos, Rowena McNulty, Jasmine McQuay, Pam Meistrich, TR Rathjen, Fran Tacoma, Michele Toscano, and Cori Uray.

As a team, we are equally blessed to work with an incredible group of client teachers and administrators who make the *Learner-Active, Technology-Infused Classroom* a reality every day. Your stories, excitement, challenges, and accomplishments provide a context through which others can envision powerful classrooms and schools.

Thanks to my high-school friend Carrie Cantor, who, to my good fortune, became a highly skilled and talented content editor. Your help in fine-tuning the content presentation of the manuscript was invaluable.

Thanks to the Boonton Breakfast Club for your unwavering support; Linda Gloshinski, for keeping me well fed with meatballs and other delicacies during my writing; Dianne Mayberry-Hatt, for reading and reading and re-reading; and Sophia Bosco, an amazing seven-year-old, for reminding me through your love of learning why this work is so important.

About the Author

Nancy Sulla is the founder and President of IDE Corp. (Innovative Designs for Education), an educational consulting company specializing in instructional and organizational design. She holds a B.A. in Education from Fairleigh Dickinson University, an M.A. in computer science from Montclair State University, and an Ed.D. in Educational Administration from Fordham University. Her diverse background includes teaching at the elementary, middle, high school, and college levels; working as a computer programmer and systems analyst; and leading teachers as a district administrator prior to launching IDE Corp. Her consulting work focuses on helping educators design *Learner-Active, Technology-Infused Classrooms*™ that engage all students in an academically rigorous, differentiated learning environment, in which they take responsibility for their own learning.

Introduction

"It was the best of times, it was the worst of times, it was the age of wisdom, it was the age of foolishness, it was the epoch of belief, it was the epoch of incredulity. . . ." Perhaps Charles Dickens presented a foreshadowing for education and the introduction of the Common Core State Standards (CCSS) in his 1859 novel, *A Tale of Two Cities*. The "penning," or in this case "digital creating," of a set of standards that can be reviewed, printed out, and institutionalized, set the educational world in a tailspin. States started pumping out curriculum models for teachers to follow, school districts started aligning their classroom curriculum with the standards, and teachers started writing the numbers and letters of the standards in their plan books. The CCSS, however, were intended to be a pathway to success throughout life, not a checklist of content to master for the test. The CCSS hold great promise for the future of education as they seek to ensure that students are prepared for college, career, and life. When approached through that lens, they can represent the best of times: an age of wisdom and an epoch of belief that schools can actually chart a course for the future of a nation and, in fact, the world.

Advancing a Nation, the World

In 2009, the CCSS were born of a joint effort between the National Governors Association Center for Best Practices and the Council of Chief State School Officers. The purpose of the CCSS is to define a set of expectations as to what students should know and be able to do as a result of K–12 schooling, regardless of the school attended. The premise is that, if achieved, these standards will ensure that students will be well prepared for college, career, and life. They offer up a robust, and yet reasonable, set of expectations to guide curriculum developers, instructional designers, and teachers. Most importantly, they offer an important future focus: preparing students for life beyond the K–12 experience.

The introduction to the CCSS mathematics standards states: "The standards encourage students to solve real-world problems" (http://www.corestandards.org/Math/). The introduction to the CCSS English language arts standards states that the standards stress "critical thinking, problem-solving, and analytical skills that are required for success in college, career, and life" (http://www.corestandards.org/ELA-Literacy/). This new, powerful set of standards seeks to position the U.S. to be globally competitive. A significant part of that preparation is the ability to find and solve real-world, complex, open-ended problems. The standards also seek to ensure that students around the country experience a commonality of learning outcomes, strengthening a national mindset in a world in which people move easily and regularly from state to state.

At this time in our nation's history, we find ourselves part of a global economy, environment, and civilization with countries inextricably linked to one another. (This was not the case in 1635 when the first U.S. public school was established.) Preparing students for their future, and in fact, charting a course for the future, requires much different thinking today than that of 400 years ago. The CCSS offer a blueprint for re-culturing schools to serve a global society; however, schools must keep their eye on the future and not merely on a set of printed standards. *It's Not What You Teach But How* moves beyond curricular content to re-thinking the very practices found inside classrooms, with the goal of designing classrooms that better prepare students to succeed, thrive in, and chart the course of our global society.

Two Words

The CCSS can be summed up in two words: *understanding* and *application*. They challenge students and their teachers to push beyond short-term content acquisition and rote mastery of procedures to levels of thinking that result in continual learning and real-world problem solving. They are purposefully designed to prepare students to succeed in life beyond the K–12 experience.

The first word of many of the math content standards is "understand." For example, a kindergarten math standard states:

> Understand that the last number name said tells the number of objects counted.

It's not enough for a child to walk upstairs counting, "one, two, three, four. . . ." When the child stops with "fourteen" at the top, he must understand that that number represents the quantity, or total number, of stairs he just climbed; he must have a concept of fourteen.

A fourth-grade math standard states:

Understand a fraction a/b as a multiple of 1/b.

The student must understand that three-fourths is the value one-fourth taken 3 times, thus a multiple of one-fourth. Coloring in fraction parts and computing with fractions does not equate to understanding the concept of fractions. Understanding requires significant engagement with concrete examples and real-world situations in which the student experiences personal "aha" moments.

A high-school statistics and probability standard states:

Understand statistics as a process for making inferences about population parameters based on a random sample from that population.

It is not enough to know the various statistical calculations or to follow the process laid out by the teacher or textbook; students must understand the purpose and power of statistics. They must engage with statistical problems that make sense to them so that they see the connections, make inferences, and test hypotheses.

A fourth-grade writing standard states:

Use concrete words and phrases and sensory details to convey experiences and events precisely.

Students must possess an understanding of concrete words and phrases and sensory details in order to use them. However, the standard focuses on the end-goal of enhanced communication, which requires the application of an understanding of concrete words and phrases and sensory details.

A high-school informational text standard states:

Delineate and evaluate the argument and specific claims in a text, assessing whether the reasoning is valid and the evidence is relevant and sufficient; identify false statements and fallacious reasoning.

Here, students must understand the concept and skill of reasoning in order to evaluate it; they must understand the concepts of evidence, relevance, and sufficiency in order to achieve the standard. Armed with a deep understanding of those concepts and skills, students can tackle any number of situations requiring argument evaluation.

While it used to be that teachers could feel accomplished by teaching the lesson and having students practice, today, building understanding and application requires significant student engagement with content and active participation in the learning process.

Mere memorization may last a lifetime yet have little bearing on future problem finding. Many years after high-school graduation, adults may harken back to using mnemonic devices to remember that the formula for tangent in trigonometry is opposite over adjacent; but without understanding, that knowledge cannot serve them throughout their lives. The power of K–12 content to shape the future of students' lives and the world depends upon students' ability to understand it.

From Understanding to Application

Understanding leads to successful application, and the CCSS frequently present content through its application. A second-grade speaking and listening standard challenges students to:

> Build on others' talk in conversations by linking their comments to the remarks of others.

Students must demonstrate an understanding of what their peers are saying in order to apply their knowledge of responding with their own, related comments. Absent of an understanding of the process of listening and comprehending someone's comments, and then linking one's own ideas to them, the student will not be able to effectively engage in conversation.

A fifth-grade literature standard challenges students to:

> Determine a theme of a story . . . from details in the text. . . .

Here, students must first understand what a detail is and then understand the details themselves in order to determine a theme. Absent of that understanding, the student will fall short of the standard's expectation. Following a teacher's demonstration or process alone will not produce the necessary level of understanding. That's not to say teachers' demonstrations and lessons are not necessary; they are. However, in addition to direct instruction, students must engage with content to build a level of understanding that will arm them with the skills they need to apply the standards in a variety of situations.

A high-school writing standard challenges students to:

> Produce clear and coherent writing in which the development, organization, and style are appropriate to task, purpose, and audience.

Students must apply an understanding of task, purpose, and audience in developing their writing, and also apply an understanding of development, organization, and style of writing.

In 2006, school technology director Karl Fisch produced his first musically enhanced, digital slideshow on the influence technology was having around the globe that would have an impact on teachers in his school; the video was titled *Shift Happens*, later renamed *Did You Know*. His statistics stunned viewers into a new world view: "India has more honors kids than the US has kids. . . . Today's learner will have 10 to 14 jobs before the age of 38." The videos went viral and became poignant presentations shown at school professional development days, emailed to colleagues, and discussed at faculty room tables. Most compelling was the statement that, "We are currently preparing students for jobs that don't yet exist, using technologies that haven't yet been invented, in order to solve problems we don't even know are problems yet." The CCSS seek to prepare students to succeed and thrive in that reality.

The End of Teacher–Proofed Curriculum

Some fear that more rigorous standards and standardized tests just cause educators to "teach to the test." Textbook publishers pump out new curricular programs (an expansion on the outdated "textbook") that claim to address these new standards and tests. Teachers implement state-designed curriculum modules page by page, hoping to yield success. None of those approaches will work. What is needed is a workforce of teachers who are empowered with content knowledge and instructional strategies that, in turn, empower students to take charge of their own learning and chart a course for their future.

As is the case with students, teachers must own a deep level of understanding of the content and expectations of the CCSS. Understanding the CCSS requires engagement with the standards and processing of the anticipated performance outcomes. The standards cannot be "delivered." Teachers must create student-centered, problem-based instructional environments that foster the level of achievement defined by the CCSS. No one can hand teachers a set of lessons that will produce success. The CCSS require deliberate and purposeful facilitation of learning. There is no "teacher proofing" of these standards. Teachers must be prepared and empowered to lead students to higher levels of thinking and content acquisition.

The Essence of the Standards Transcend All Subject Areas

The CCSS directly address only English language arts (ELA) and math, with ELA standards for history, social studies, science, and technical subjects. The essence of these standards, however, is less about specific content and more about a higher-order level of thinking in approaching content. The standards represent conceptual shifts in the outcomes of schooling, with a much greater focus on the ability to solve real-world problems than ever before. Additionally, they marry content standards with characteristics of those who are ready for college, career, and life—characteristics that transcend the disciplines. The Next Generation Science Standards (NGSS) follow suit, focusing on a higher-order, problem-solving approach to science. They, too, include crosscutting concepts that transcend the disciplines.

No matter what the subject area, you can view your course content through the lens of higher-order, real-world problem solving. As you read this book, consider the shifts in the CCSS and apply them to any content area. Additionally, literacy and numeracy are key foundations for the study of any content. Social studies students must be able to read well, comprehend, and apply higher-order thinking to master the key concepts of this subject area and be positioned to solve related real-world problems. Students of the arts must be able to read directions and critiques, write about process and reflections, and apply mathematical concepts to the field. Physical education students must be able to master cause-and-effect relationships, inference, and sequences; they would benefit from the ability to read and generate charts and graphs. No matter the subject, the CCSS apply. Throughout the book, I will include references to various disciplines outside of ELA and math. I encourage you, the reader, to view the book as a template through which you can consider any content area.

Seven Insights

This book will focus on the *how* of teaching, taking into account the *what* of the CCSS. Focusing on what the standards say can cause you to miss some key elements in achieving them. Each chapter of the book will offer you an insight to explore and strategies to implement:

1. **CCSS Achievement Requires Ends-Based Teaching.** The CCSS are written as a set of "ends," the result of the teaching/learning relationship. This chapter will provide strategies for designing classrooms that focus on the ends rather than merely on the means, which could result in missing the ends altogether.

2. **Understanding Requires Grappling.** Teach in ways that produce not just knowledge acquisition, but deep understanding that leads to application. Building understanding requires the learner to "grapple" with content in a structured environment that provides motivation, probing of thinking, and leveled support. This chapter will offer strategies for building understanding through grappling.

3. **Cognitive Progression Is a Lever for Achievement.** While that sounds like a mouthful, it means that if you understand how the brain learns, you can leverage that knowledge to produce results. You've most likely experienced situations in which you were so overwhelmed by the content you could barely learn anything, and situations in which you were bored because you already possessed the knowledge being presented. This chapter will provide strategies for how to use cognitive science to produce results.

4. **The Power of Language Transcends the Disciplines.** Language has the power to change lives and the world. Every subject area can be viewed as a language and taught as such. For example, math is the language used to describe the natural world. This chapter will offer strategies for focusing on the power of language across the disciplines.

5. **Executive Function Is Foundational for All Learning.** Without executive function, you cannot achieve the level of mastery required by the CCSS. Children growing up under stressful conditions do not always build adequate executive function to succeed in their academic studies. This chapter will promote a deeper understanding of executive function and offer strategies for building a learning environment that focuses on both academics and executive function.

6. **Purposeful Instruction Yields Retention.** The CCSS do not address how to acquire new knowledge nor how to motivate students to learn a given skill, concept, or piece of information. That's what this book is about. This chapter introduces the learning hourglass of three stages of learning—motivation, acquisition, and retention—and

proposes a difference between learning and practice activities. This chapter will offer strategies for teaching a student, as opposed to a lesson, and, thus, for differentiating instruction toward learning retention.

7. CCSS Achievement Relies on Teacher Facilitation. Facilitation toward application is more than responding to students' needs and questions. This chapter will offer strategies for practicing powerful facilitation to achieve the level of understanding and application required by the CCSS.

Each insight focuses on helping students master the skills, concepts, and habits they will need to thrive beyond their K–12 experience: in college, career, and life. The objective of *It's Not What You Teach But How* is to maximize the interconnectedness of the CCSS, the actions teachers take, and the resultant student learning—and, in the process, to design classrooms for a new age in the history of education.

The final chapter offers a look at a comprehensive classroom model that can be used to address the *how* of teaching, outlined in my first book, *Students Taking Charge: Inside the Learner-Active, Technology-Infused Classroom*. This chapter will describe how this model addresses the levels of achievement demanded by the CCSS.

Along the way, you'll find "Your Turn" opportunities to grapple with the content of this book and design materials to use in classrooms. The future may not be easily defined, but it can be shaped by masterful teachers who are right now preparing the next generation of world citizens.

Chapter 1

Problem-Finders, Innovators, and Entrepreneurs

The future is not Google-able.

—*William Gibson*

Our lives are changing at an unprecedented pace. Transformational shifts in our economic, environmental, geopolitical, societal and technological systems offer unparalleled opportunities, but the interconnections among them also imply enhanced systemic risks. Stakeholders from across business, government and civil society face an evolving imperative in understanding and managing emerging global risks which, by definition, respect no national boundaries.

(World Economic Forum, 2014, p. 7)

Thomas Friedman (2007) asserted that the world is flat. Technology has created one global society, melding individuals and companies in different countries, allowing employees of one company to work from anywhere in the world, and fostering communication and collaboration among peoples around the world. This flattening offers the "empowerment of individuals to act globally" (Friedman, 2007, p. 11). Even work challenges and government policies that seem to be local may have global impact. We no longer depend solely on our own community or country; we are all intertwined; we are a global society. More than sharing information, we solve problems with people around the world, whether a problem is addressing a supply-and-demand issue for goods, collaborating on space exploration or environmental issues, utilizing available personnel for help-desk issues, or averting war. Likewise, we create problems for one another around the world based on actions we take in our own countries that affect the economy, environment, and humanity.

Figure 1.1 Solve for X (www.solveforx.com) Key Graphic

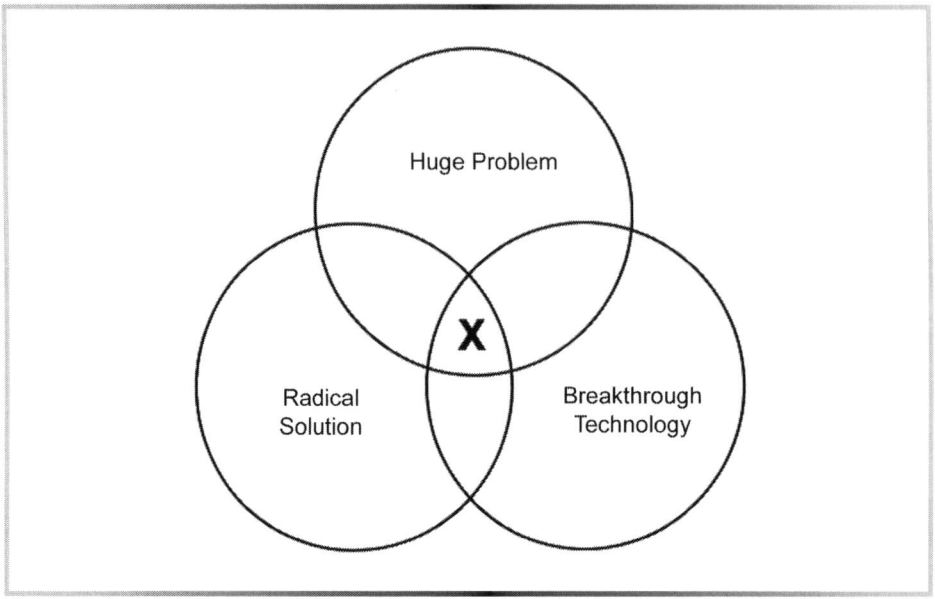

In February of 2012, *Google* held an experimental event over three days during which "forty-six scientists, entrepreneurs and innovators from around the world came together to discuss and debate radical solutions using breakthrough technologies to some really big problems" (www. solveforx.com/about/team). As a result, *Google* launched a website called "Solve for X" (www.solveforx.com): "A place to hear about and discuss radical technology ideas for solving global problems." A key site graphic (see Figure 1.1) defines "moonshot thinking" through three intersecting circles marked "huge problem," "radical solution," and "breakthrough technology," with the intersection being marked "x." The site offers videos of "Solve for X" talks, opportunities for the public to digitally discuss issues, and the ability to create circles of people interested in the same problems for the purpose of collaboration.

One "Solve for X" video describes thirty-something Leslie Dewan's innovation for producing energy from nuclear waste. At the time of her "moonshot thinking," the world had amassed 270,000 metric tons of high-level nuclear waste—a number that was continuing to build at 9,000 metric tons per year. She and colleague Mark Massie designed the "Waste-Annihilating Molten Salt Reactor," which would convert nuclear waste into electricity. Given 270,000 metric tons of nuclear waste, they predict the reactor could produce enough electricity to power the world for seventy-two years.

Leslie and Mark were Ph.D. students at M.I.T. when they decided to take the next step beyond academia and design a nuclear reactor. They considered that the nuclear waste from a typical nuclear reactor still contained significant energy and determined that they should find a way to extract the remaining energy: problem-finders who went beyond the typical question of simply how to *store* nuclear waste to how to eliminate it. They won the U.S. Department of Energy's top award in the Future Energy innovation contest: innovators who developed a unique solution to a global problem. They decided to build these reactors: entrepreneurs who started a company called Transatomic.

In another Solve for X video, Aldo Steinfeld shares his "aha" moment flying from Germany to California in which he realized that, based on the amount of fuel consumed by the jet and the number of passengers on the plane, his carbon footprint for that flight was 1.4 tons of CO_2. A problem-finder sets the stage for innovation. Given there were then no alternative fuels for aircraft, his "moonshot thinking" became how to produce airplane fuel from water, CO_2, and solar energy. An innovator generates new ideas and fuels the drive for entrepreneurship. As an entrepreneur, Aldo heads the Solar Technology Laboratory at the Paul Scherrer Institute in Zurich, where this idea can come to fruition.

A third Solve for X video shows Dr. Keith Black sharing his "moonshot thinking" for identifying beta amyloid plaques building up in the brain—the building blocks of Alzheimer's—through an eye examination. His radical solution would allow people to take significant steps early on to slow the advancement of the disease. Dr. Black knew that pharmaceuticals existed to treat the brain for the plaque buildup. As a problem-finder, he recognized the need to identify the existence of these plaques well in advance of the appearance of the disease's symptoms, at which point a significant loss of brain cells would have already occurred. As an innovator, he designed a retinal imaging test to accomplish just that. As an entrepreneur, he co-founded NeuroVision Imaging, LLC to develop the capability to perform the test.

Problem–Finders

In a world in which we have to solve problems we don't even know are problems yet, problem finding is an important next step beyond the solving of known problems. Problem-finders:

> . . . sort through vast amounts of information and inputs, often
> from multiple disciplines; experiment with a variety of different

approaches; are willing to switch directions in the course of a project; and often take longer than their counterparts to complete their work.

(Pink, 2012, p. 127)

Perhaps the first reference to problem-finders was made in 1881 by the French philosopher Paul Souriau, as cited by Sawyer (2006, p. 72): "There is something mechanical, as it were, in the art of finding solutions. The truly original mind is that which finds problems." While Souriau drew attention to the power of problem finding, it appears the term "problem-finder" was first introduced in a study of creativity by Getzels and Csikszentmihalyi (1976). They identified two stages of problem finding: problem formulation and problem solution. They noted, too, that problem finding is not a skill relegated to a talented, creative few; the creativity required for problem finding is more a matter of connecting with purpose than of possessing any particular skillset.

Children can be taught to be problem-finders. More recently, Ewan McIntosh gave a Ted Talk in which he proposed that schools place an emphasis on problem finding, beyond the current focus on problem solving. Teachers who offer students a field of content in which to find and solve problems are developing problem-finders. A global society that must be prepared to solve problems it doesn't even know are problems yet needs problem-finders. Schools must produce problem-finders.

Innovators

In a society that has moved from an agrarian economic model to an industrial model to an information model, we need "a new engine of economic growth for the twenty-first century. . . . And there is general agreement as to what that new economy must be based on. One word: innovators" (Wagner, 2012, p. 2). According to www.oxforddictionaries.com, an innovator is "a person who introduces new methods, ideas, or products." Innovators associate, question, observe, experiment, and network (Wagner, 2012).

Stanford University is home to the ground-breaking d.school (the Hasso Plattner Institute of Design) in which students apply "design thinking" and focus on "how to ease people's lives." As a result of their work, students have "developed original ways to tackle infant mortality, unreliable electricity and malnutrition in the third world" (Perlroth, 2013, p. 1); d.school is developing innovators. Teachers who engage students in devising solutions for open-ended, authentic problems are developing innovators. The future of a country's economy and success as a world leader depends upon the work of innovators. Schools must produce innovators.

Entrepreneurs

Innovators who turn ideas into action are entrepreneurs. The word "entrepreneur" derives from the early 19th century French term *entreprendre*, to undertake. Yong Zhao (2012) asserts that we need to broaden the use of the term entrepreneur as it applies to today's society. In the traditional sense, entrepreneurs create jobs for themselves by starting businesses or supplying goods or services. Not all entrepreneurs need own their own business, however; they need only turn their ideas into action. Social entrepreneurs seek to make a difference through the promotion of social values: making a difference in the world that does not necessarily translate into personal profit. Entrepreneurship follows innovation: where innovation is the having of new ideas, entrepreneurship is the enacting of those ideas. Both rely on problem finding and innovation. Teachers who provide students with opportunities to engage with real audiences and turn their ideas into action are developing entrepreneurs. A civilization that intends to progress over time, and not vanish, requires entrepreneurs. Schools must produce entrepreneurs.

Tomorrow's Moonshot Thinkers

Clearly, if we fail to identify and solve the world's biggest problems, nothing else will really matter. It is likely that most of those "moonshot thinkers" who will, in fact, identify and offer viable solutions to global problems are sitting in classrooms today; perhaps some are sitting in classrooms in your school. If these problem-finders, innovators, and entrepreneurs seem like they will only emerge from among the gifted and talented students, look again. A sixth-grade student read a book on airplane engines and wrote to the Pentagon, suggesting ideas for making its fighter planes more efficient and effective; the Pentagon wrote back. Students living in a town where a new bridge is under construction learned that a plan for connecting a pedestrian/bike path had not yet been devised. They set to work researching and offering innovative ideas, which they presented to the bridge project leaders. These are just two examples of many classroom projects in which students were charged with making a difference.

In order for schools to meet the needs of a global society, they must prepare students to be problem-finders, innovators, and entrepreneurs. None of these skills should be viewed as innate; they all can be taught, to all students, at varying levels. Today's students are ready to make the leap from passive recipients of information to active participants in a classroom that will prepare them for their future. The world needs problem-finders, innovators, and entrepreneurs.

What Today's Employers Want

When it comes to the needs of employers, if a picture says a thousand words, then the word cloud in Figure 1.2 says it all. As part of a regional research initiative, *WorkForce Now* (Regional Economic Research Institute, 2013), three major employers in Southwest Florida (Arthrex, Chico's, and Lee Memorial Health System) were asked to provide information on their critical employment gaps—positions that are difficult to fill for lack of qualified employees. They shared the job descriptions and requirements of these positions. Feeding these job descriptions and requirements into www.wordle.net—an online tool that calculates the frequency of words and displays them in a font size relative to their frequency—produced this image.

Note that the greatest needs of these employers are for those who communicate well, possess a customer service orientation, solve problems, act well as team players, and utilize technology. An online survey of 318 employers concurs, indicating that 93% value critical thinking, communication, and complex problem-solving skills over a candidate's undergraduate degree (Hart Research Associates, 2013). "More than three in four employees say they want colleges to place more emphasis on helping students develop five key learning outcomes, including: critical thinking, complex problem solving, written and oral communication, and applied knowledge in real-world settings" (p. 1). Additionally, the survey revealed that an employee's ability to contribute to the innovation of a company is a high priority for employers. Whereas schools have been criticized for failing to produce a skilled and knowledgeable workforce for today's society (Carnevale, 2013), the CCSS now address all of these skills.

Figure 1.2 Wordle Created From Employer Needs

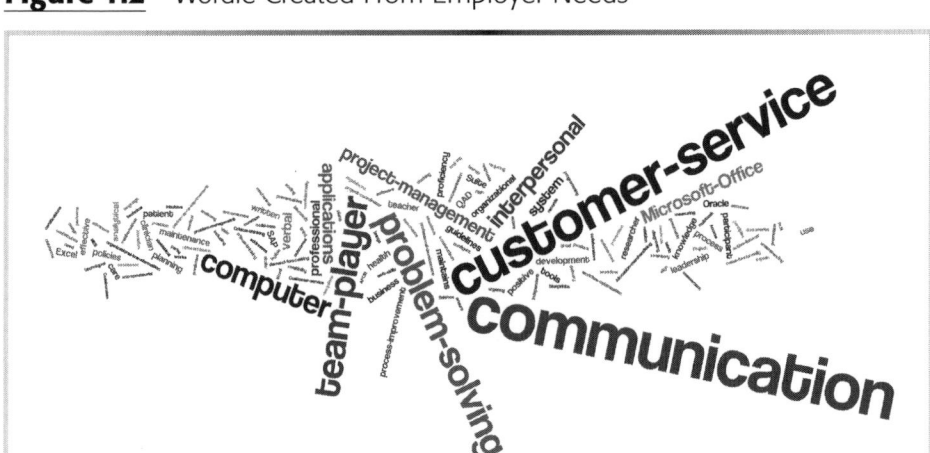

Educating Problem-Finders, Innovators, and Entrepreneurs

Much of the information schools have spent years having students memorize is now all available on the Internet: "Google-able," if you will. However, while facts, data, and other information are available, what are not are the solutions to complex, real-world problems and, more importantly, the finding of problems. As the novelist William Gibson said, "The future is not Google-able" (comment made at A Clean Well-Lighted Place for Books, Feb. 5, 2004).

In an online *Forbes* magazine article entitled, "Educate for problem-solving, not factories" (Townsend, 2012), the author asserts that educators "must consider the power of new learning models to unlock the potential of youth . . . create value by teaching people to make a living as problem-solvers and purposeful entrepreneurs" (par. 18). While computers can automate many rote-skill jobs—such as tollbooth collectors, bank tellers, grocery clerks, etc.—complex problem finding and problem solving is still largely a human process.

Yong Zhao, in his 2012 book *World Class Learners: Educating Creative and Entrepreneurial Students,* drives home the need to educate students to innovate and, from their ideas, take action. Zhao shares bold ideas by those who are studying this entrepreneurial phenomena: "Entrepreneurs are believed to have more power to solve the complex problems facing human beings and bring prosperity to humanity than governments and international organizations" (Zhao, 2012, p. 4). Serving society means helping students foster entrepreneurial thinking, the kind of thinking exhibited by global problem-solvers.

In 2005, Dale Dougherty first published *Make* magazine for those who like to, simply put, make things. He called his subscribers "makers," and the result was the creation of a subculture of entrepreneurial, technology-driven, do-it-yourselfers who problem-find, innovate, share ideas, collaborate, and attend Maker Faires. This publication essentially launched the Maker Movement. In 2011, Dale was honored by the White House as a "Champion of Change" for tapping into the innate desire of people to take control over their lives and the tools they use, empowering people through a like-minded community to invent.

The Maker Movement fosters problem-finders, innovators, and entrepreneurs. That same innate desire to take control of one's life exists in students today. Classrooms that encourage students to take control of their own learning and provide the structure and scaffolding to do so can produce the level of achievement required by the CCSS and the qualities to play a significant role in their future and the future of the world.

New Territory: Procedural Automaticity vs. "Novelity"

Schools serve society by *what* they teach; they form society by *how* they teach (Sulla, 2011). In order for schools to address this changing world and develop problem-finders, innovators, and entrepreneurs, schools must rethink not only *what* they teach, but *how* they teach. Critical thinking, communication, and problem solving are more about how students engage in learning than what content is being presented. The CCSS address skills and concepts typically taught in school, but they present significant shifts in the teaching-learning process. One shift is from memorization and acquisition through procedural automaticity to understanding and application.

When a teacher presents the process through which to solve a math problem, carry out a science experiment, identify the plot line of a novel, mix paint colors, serve a volleyball, interpret a population pyramid, convert music to a different scale, and so forth, students are engaging in procedural learning. They can watch the process, take notes on it, study it, enact it, and practice it. The goal is procedural automaticity. (Note, this is not the same as automaticity of math facts, requiring memorization, which is critical to success in mathematics.) Procedural automaticity is the memorization of a set of steps leading to the ability to implement a procedure automatically to produce a result, regardless of level of understanding.

To date, much of schooling has ended in procedural automaticity. One can build procedural automaticity for myriad skills: identifying the main idea, calculating the surface area, citing evidence, playing the notes of a scale, balancing chemical equations, decoding a word, conjugating a verb, shooting a basket, and so forth. A teacher presents information and models it, then has the students practice with guidance, then has them practice on their own; and, over time, they build procedural automaticity. Typical standardized tests in schools have assessed procedural automaticity. Students are presented with much the same situations they've encountered in their studies: compute these numbers, identify the main idea, calculate the area, balance the chemical equation, and so forth.

While this process may produce results on a test that offers the same types of questions as were practiced, it does not ensure understanding. It also does not ensure long-term retention, which results in teachers being faced with students who fail to remember content that was clearly addressed in prior years. With the CCSS designed to build upon learning of the prior years, educators can no longer afford to rely on procedural automaticity. Procedural automaticity is appropriate for a factory-based society, but not for a society seeking to become or remain a thought leader and innovator.

The shift in the CCSS and new standardized tests is away from rewarding mere procedural automaticity toward ensuring that students understand and can apply knowledge. What counts is what I refer to as "novelity"—the ability to respond appropriately and successfully to novel situations. Without understanding, you cannot solve problems for which there are not known solutions. Procedural automaticity won't get you there. As standardized tests are evolving, fewer questions address procedural automaticity, and more are assessing novelity. This does not mean procedural automaticity is not needed: it is a necessary but not sufficient component of preparing students for their future. Procedural automaticity can be a means to the greater end of novelity.

When I was first learning to drive, a friend of mine owned a car with a manual transmission. I wanted to learn how to drive a stick shift, and he agreed to teach me. He didn't take the usual approach, which would be to model the process of shifting and then put me behind the wheel, coaching me through it. Instead, he sat down with paper and pen and drew the driveshaft of a car. He drew and discussed with me what would happen when I depressed the clutch, changed a gear, and so forth. I engaged with the image and my mentor by asking questions and posing "what if" situations. I was able to visualize it and understand how the shifting process worked. Once I took the wheel, I hardly needed coaching because I possessed understanding. When faced with a challenge, such as a hill, I was able to figure out what steps to take, because I understood how the gears worked and could apply that understanding; I had achieved a level of "novelity." Following a procedure only works until the situation changes and one is required to think through an alternate route. Understanding yields success in many situations.

This shift to novelity requires developing a mindset of preparing students for next Tuesday's test, but not just for next Tuesday's test. Let's begin by thinking about the future for which we are preparing our students and consider how we can accomplish that in classrooms across the country, across the world.

To prepare students for an unknown future, schools must arm them with skills that transcend time and an understanding of content that can be applied to new situations as they arise. The CCSS provide a strong guide for those who wish to teach for novelity.

The Intent of the CCSS: Beyond Content

Understanding and application of content form an important foundation for life; however, subject-area content alone is not sufficient for ultimate success in college, career, and life. The ELA standards offer seven characteristics of

Table 1.1 CCSS ELA College and Career Readiness Characteristics

CCSS College and Career Readiness Characteristics	Fostered by a Learning Environment in Which Students Are . . .
Demonstrate independence	. . . taught and encouraged to self-assess, set goals, select resources, and take responsibility for their own learning
Build strong content knowledge	. . . regularly engaging with content and applying it to new situations, both independently and collaboratively, with and without the teacher's overt guidance
Respond to the varying demands of audience, task, purpose, and discipline	. . . offered ample opportunities to present to varied audiences, both verbally and in writing, around a variety of issues across the disciplines
Comprehend as well as critique	. . . asked to critique opinions, solutions, ideas, and works created by others and themselves
Value evidence	. . . encouraged to provide and demand evidence to back up claims
Use technology and digital media strategically and capably	. . . offered ample opportunities to utilize technology and digital media in the course of their studies, not as an end unto itself, but as a means to the greater end presented by the subject-area content
Come to understand other perspectives and cultures	. . . encouraged to see situations from the perspectives of others, including those around the world

students who are "College and Career Ready in Reading, Writing, Speaking, Listening, and Language." These characteristics are not specifically connected to any particular content; teachers across the content areas must offer active practice in them while pursuing content goals. This speaks of a classroom environment in which students are engaged in grappling with content, individually and collaboratively; questioning and sharing; taking responsibility for their own learning; selecting appropriate resources for learning; and relying on the teacher as a guide and a key resource in the learning process. The development of these seven characteristics will depend largely on *how* you teach. Consider for each of these characteristics the possibilities for achieving it through *how* one teaches (see Table 1.1).

A teacher can present the concept of evidence to students and demonstrate the skill of locating evidence for a claim. Students can take notes and follow up with practice. If students fail to assimilate the valuing of evidence into their lives, however, they will be ill prepared to handle yet-unknown

Table 1.2 CCSS Math Practice Standards

CCSS Mathematical Practice Standards	Fostered by a Learning Environment in Which Students Are . . .
Make sense of problems and persevere in solving them	. . . provided with problem solving on a regular basis, encouraged to work through to success, and acknowledged and celebrated for doing so
Reason abstractly and quantitatively	. . . often asked to deconstruct a problem and draw logical conclusions
Construct viable arguments and critique the reasoning of others	. . . often asked to present an argument related to content and evaluate the reasoning of their peers and others
Model with mathematics	. . . provided with manipulatives, strategies, and computer applications to model real-world situations through mathematics
Use appropriate tools strategically	. . . expected to use the tools of mathematics to present, deconstruct, and create information
Attend to precision	. . . expected to be precise in their thinking and communication
Look for and make use of structure	. . . provided with regular opportunities to examine structure within the content area
Look for and express regularity in repeated reasoning	. . . often asked to take their reasoning to the next level and explore the value of repeated reasoning

situations they might meet in their future. To prepare students for their future, teachers will need to regularly respond to students' assertions with the question, "What evidence can you show me?" and encourage students to challenge others, including the teacher, for evidence of their claims. This intentional practice would extend well beyond the lesson on evidence, with students being challenged to provide and require evidence of claims in all situations. The *how* of teaching, in this case, produces students who value evidence, and that skill will serve them well in their future.

Responding to the varying demands of audience, task, purpose, and discipline is not a unit of study; it is a skill that is developed through repeated opportunities to speak and write on myriad topics for real audiences. Success in the college and career readiness standards emerges from the *how* of teaching more than the *what*.

The mathematics standards introduce eight standards for mathematical practice that outline the habits required for achievement, provided in Table 1.2.

As with the college and career readiness characteristics, these habits reach beyond specific content mastery; they are evident across the content areas and in many life situations. While they may be explained, they are not achieved through lessons in the classroom; they are achieved through the culture of the classroom, the *how* of teaching. Attention to precision is not a unit of study, it is an expectation modeled and held in high regard by teachers all throughout the year, regardless of assignment or activity.

Perseverance is not a content lesson, it is a habit built through an intentional classroom culture that places an emphasis on it, with the teacher encouraging students to stick with a problem or process and seeing it through to completion in spite of the challenges. That's the *how* of teaching.

Teaching with the *how* in mind means building a classroom culture that cultivates these seven characteristics and eight habits. As students build these characteristics and habits, they will excel in their content-related studies. A classroom of independent learners who persevere in problem solving and attend to precision can make any teacher's work easier.

Standards-Based Teaching

While the CCSS do not define *how* to teach, their very nature offers a guide for teaching techniques. Students build understanding and application through problem solving and deliberate and purposeful engagement with content; through personal investment and responsibility for their own learning; through the relentless pursuit of ideas and questions that are of interest to them; and through access to a variety of resources, including the teacher. These are the characteristics of problem-finders, innovators, and entrepreneurs. Standards-based teaching isn't simply about providing lessons on specific standards. It's about developing a classroom environment through which students will come to learn, achieving a high level of understanding necessary for the application of knowledge.

The insights presented in the subsequent chapters of this book will provide strategies for deconstructing the standards and building a deeper understanding of them. Just as students need to gain an understanding of the content of the standards in order to apply them throughout life, educators need to gain an understanding of the standards themselves in order to apply them in their work. Most districts have aligned their curriculum to the CCSS, meaning they've ensured that the skills and concepts are represented; however, ensuring that students attain the level of mastery outlined in the CCSS requires realigning the teaching-learning process.

Positioning students to be problem-finders, innovators, and entrepreneurs in order to thrive in their future requires creating learning environments through which students gain more than a cursory knowledge of content. Teaching today requires keeping an eye on the future and intentionally designing learning experiences aimed at producing specific results, with the end-goal being understanding; understanding is developed through grappling.

Chapter 2

The First Insight

CCSS Achievement Requires Ends–Based Teaching

Simplicity is ultimately a matter of focus.

—Ann Voskamp

In the early days of formal education, learning to read was deemed to be a necessary skill. Someone or some group of educators then deconstructed reading, determining that to understand text, one had to first be able to comprehend a sentence. To accomplish that, one had to comprehend a word. To accomplish that, one had to decode a word. To accomplish that, one had to know letter sounds. Early reading instruction was then based largely on phonics and decoding words. The teacher may have known that the end goal was reading a book, but for the student, the means was put before the end. Children were instructed in letter and word recognition, and then sentence comprehension, without the deliberate connection to reading books. Ideally, though, students should have both.

Over time, literacy instruction has evolved to encourage more early student encounters with books and discussions of book content, if only through pictures, while students learn decoding skills. However, even as of the writing of this book, the instructional focus is still largely on the means rather than the end goal of reading.

This flawed practice of putting the means before the end is prevalent in core content classes. In math class, students learn about prime and composite numbers. The numbers 1, 2, 3, 5, and 7, for example, are prime, meaning that they cannot be divided any further into whole numbers beyond themselves and one. The numbers 4, 6, and 8 are composite, or made up of multiples of prime numbers; they can be further divided into smaller whole numbers. From here, students learn how to factor numbers to their primes, so 8 becomes 2 × 2 × 2, and 12 becomes 2 × 2 × 3. Then students learn how to identify the Greatest Common Factor of two numbers. Since 8 and 12 both have 2 × 2 in common among their prime factors, their Greatest Common Factor is 4. Next, students consider the fraction 8/12. To reduce the fraction to its lowest terms, making it easier to comprehend, they divide both the numerator and denominator by the Greatest Common Factor, or 4, arriving at 2/3. This is the route to reducing a fraction to its lowest terms.

Prime and composite numbers are critical concepts for students; however, they are only meaningful, in this case, in the context of efficiently naming amounts using fractions. How many students realize that that's where they're headed when they're first introduced to prime numbers? Probably few, if any. The end goal is reducing fractions to lowest terms so they are easier to comprehend. Using the Greatest Common Factor is a strategy for reducing fractions to lowest terms, which requires the strategy of factoring numbers, which requires the strategy of identifying a prime number.

Brain researcher David Sousa (2005) demonstrated through his research that in order for information to be stored in long-term memory, it had to make sense and have meaning. Understanding the end goal is a step toward having lower-level skills and concepts make sense and have meaning. It is important to engage students in the end goal first, creating a motivation and context for learning strategies and lower-order skills in order to accomplish that end goal. This approach leads to sense-making and meaning-making, and thus greater understanding and the ability to apply learning to new situations, or "novelty." Absent of this, students may, at best, become compliant, following procedures to make the teacher happy. Distinguishing between the means and the end, and addressing each with the appropriate intent, will yield greater success in achieving the CCSS.

Ends–Based Teaching

There is a difference between knowing something and teaching it. Let's return to my story from chapter 1 of learning how to drive a car with a manual transmission. My friend knew how to drive and he knew the nuances of when to shift, when to skip a gear, how to shift for traveling up or down a hill, the speed at which he'd have to be moving to downshift, and so forth. When teaching me how to drive, however, he started with the statement: the objective is to get the car moving smoothly without destroying my clutch or blowing up the engine. That objective got to the heart of what counted; it represented the end goal. All of my friend's explanations and questions related back to this objective; all of my questions did as well. We would discuss what made shifting smooth and why, how a clutch could burn out, and how an engine can blow. If the skill of driving a car with a manual transmission were a standard, it might read:

> Draw on knowledge of the interactions among the clutch, gearshift, and gas pedal to ensure the smooth shifting of gears that turn a driveshaft in order to drive a car with a manual transmission efficiently and effectively.

My friend got right to the essence of the standard: drive efficiently and effectively. His subsequent instruction focused on achieving that objective. By narrowing the focus of his instruction, however, he allowed me to maximize the impact of those other words. As my driving mentor talked about letting up on the gas, I could think, "If I do that for too long, I might stall, so there must be an optimal amount of time to let up on the gas." My focus continued to be on the end goal: drive efficiently and effectively.

Given new content, the learner finds it difficult to make the necessary connections and cognitive leaps to put it all together. If my driving mentor had demonstrated how to use the clutch and how to change a gear, and then had me practice until I mastered the maneuvers, he could not assume I would understand how those maneuvers work together to some greater end. As long as I drove under similar conditions, I might be successful; but given an unknown road challenge, absent of understanding, I most likely would not be able to successfully navigate it. Because my mentor focused on the end goal of driving efficiently and effectively, every subsequent piece of information he offered me begged the question: how will that ensure a smooth and safe ride? Focusing on the end led to greater understanding.

Finding the End Goal

Reading a standard is like reading a roadmap. There is the destination; and there are one or more routes to getting there. When you read a standard, you have to be sure you're identifying the destination and not just the route(s). For example, a second-grade ELA standard for informational text states:

> Know and use various text features (e.g., captions, bold print, subheadings, glossaries, indexes, electronic menus, icons) to locate key facts or information in a text efficiently.

The goal is being able to locate key facts or information efficiently; the routes to getting there are the various text features that help the reader to uncover the facts or information. The challenge of this format is that it can be easy to begin reading the standard and, as a result, invest valuable time in teaching and assessing only the strategies—and therefore fall short of providing students with the time needed for them to apply these skills to accomplish the actual end goal of the standard. In this case, you have to read the standard backwards to get to the end goal, or essence, of it.

Without a focus on the end goal, some may read this standard and spend time teaching captions, bold print, subheadings, and so forth. They may have students practice identifying subheadings and reading glossaries, locating information in indexes, and explaining captions. However, unless they have students actively engage in regularly gleaning information from a text, using captions, bold print, subheadings, and so forth, their well-meaning efforts will fall short of achieving the standard.

The strategies mentioned in the standard are only tools for accomplishing what counts; and while students must learn these skills, they must go beyond them to achieve the standard. Teaching to the end goal does not mean foregoing the teaching of the foundational strategies. If anything, the more varied the opportunities to learn the strategies, the more likely learning will take place. However, all instruction and learning activities should connect back to the why, which is the end goal.

Figure 2.1 provides a graphic representation of the end goal and the strategies needed to achieve this particular standard. Thinking of a

Figure 2.1   Ends-Based ELA Example

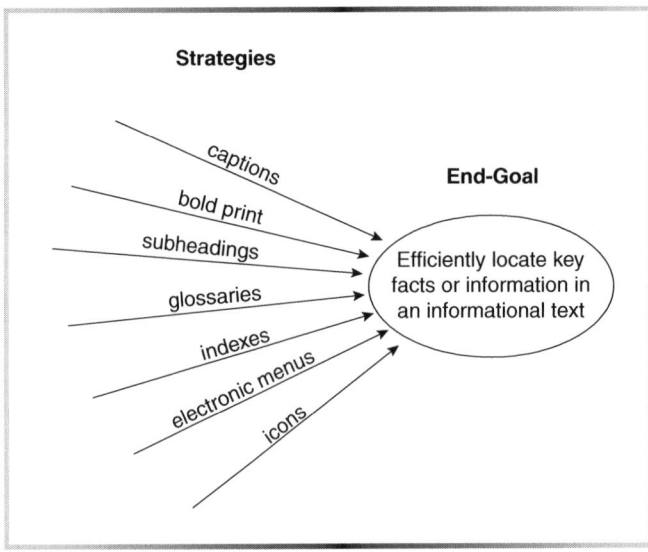

standard in this way can help you select and design appropriate instructional activities. These types of graphic depictions can help your students focus on the end goal as well.

To help students meet this particular standard, teachers might have students select a book of informational text that is of interest to them and give them ten minutes to write down the most important information. After an initial experience on their part of reading informational text, the teacher might offer repeated opportunities to learn strategies, followed by time to apply them to further reading. Each time, the teacher would have students identify how they found that information—that is, which of the strategies they used. Students might work in pairs, sharing interesting information with one another along with how they identified it. They might engage in a problem-based learning task and need to locate information from a text. The strategies of knowing how to use captions, the glossary, the index, subheadings, and so forth, will help them accomplish their task.

Prior to CCSS testing, students might have answered standardized test questions that assessed knowledge of each of those strategies independently. For example, they may have answered multiple-choice questions on definitions of the glossary, index, subheadings, etc. An effective assessment of this standard, however, would offer students a sample of informational text and instruct them to identify key information, with the expectation that they will use those strategies to do so and identify them.

Reading the standard properly will place the focus on the understanding and application aspect of the standard. Teaching with the end goal in mind, for this standard, means providing students with many opportunities to read informational text and glean key information from it, offering the foundational skills as tools in their repertoire. The CCSS are written in two formats. In some cases, strategies are stated at the beginning of the standard, and the actual end goal of the standard is stated at the end of the standard; in others, the end goal is stated at the beginning followed by strategies.

Means-to-End Standards

As with the ELA example just presented, sometimes you have to think through the standard to identify the end goal from the strategies or component parts. A fourth-grade math standard on number and operations in base 10 states:

> Multiply a whole number of up to four digits by a one-digit whole number, and multiply two two-digit numbers, using strategies based on place value and the properties of operations. Illustrate and explain the calculation by using equations, rectangular arrays, and/or area models.

Upon first glance, it appears this standard is about multiplying multi-digit numbers; and teachers could start offering lessons and providing students with practice worksheets. But note the final part of the standard: "illustrate and explain." The end goal of this standard is demonstrating an understanding of multi-digit multiplication. It's important for students to be able to multiply two numbers, but a calculator could provide that answer. It's equally, if not more, important for the student to understand multiplication, and to demonstrate that understanding by illustrating and explaining the process. That's the end goal of this standard. The strategies used to accomplish it include place value, properties of operations, equations, rectangular arrays, and area models. See Figure 2.2.

Focusing on the essence of the standard might, in this case, mean having students work in pairs to offer as many different illustrations and explanations as they can brainstorm for solving real-world problems involving multi-digit multiplication. For example, if you are trying to print copies of a book you wrote and your printer can output 22 pages per minute, how many pages can it print in an hour, or 60 minutes? Rather than merely teaching students to solve the problem, this standard requires that students think about the many ways they can represent the calculation in order to demonstrate understanding. Additionally, students can brainstorm ways in which they can use multiplication to solve problems in their everyday lives: find the problem, solve it, and explain how they solved it.

In former days, students would answer standardized test questions that have them solve multiplication problems. An effective assessment of this standard, however, would present the students with complex, real-world problems to solve through multi-digit multiplication, asking them

Figure 2.2 Ends-Based Math Example

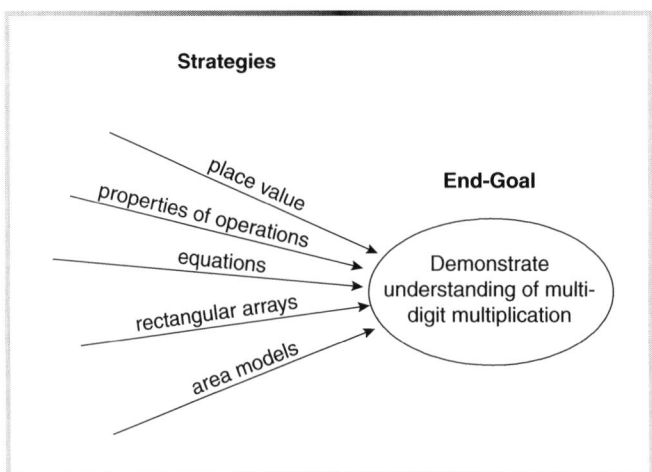

to illustrate and explain the process so that others can come to understand. Reading the standard properly will focus on the "end" of the understanding and application aspect of the standard. Providing a page filled with correctly solved problems does not necessarily equate to understanding. As is the case with the prior example, with this standard format, the end goal is at the end of the standard. The focus should be on the end goal, providing students with the strategies through which to achieve it.

Ends–to–Means Standards

The second format used by the CCSS states the end goal first, followed by the strategies. An eighth-grade ELA writing standard states:

> Develop the topic with relevant, well-chosen facts, definitions, concrete details, quotations, or other information and examples.

In this case, the end goal is to develop a topic in writing; how one accomplishes that is through using relevant, well-chosen facts, definitions, concrete details, and so forth. Addressing the end goal requires providing students with ample and diverse opportunities to write in order to develop a topic, with an expectation that those strategies will be apparent in the topic development. Again, the focus must be on the effective development of a topic, not merely on the ability to string together facts, details, and quotes. They are a means to an end.

Having students spend a lot of time identifying facts, definitions, quotations, and examples on a topic, but then spend little time assembling them to develop the topic, places the emphasis on the means and not the end. Focusing on the end goal of this standard requires providing students with repeated and varied opportunities to write to develop a topic, learning and practicing the strategies while focusing on the end goal.

A first grade math standard for operations and algebra states:

> Add and subtract within 20, demonstrating fluency for addition and subtraction within 10. Use strategies such as counting on; making ten . . .; decomposing a number leading to a ten . . .; using the relationship between addition and subtraction . . .; and creating equivalent but easier or known sums. . . .

The end goal is adding and subtracting within 20, demonstrating fluency within 10. The strategies that follow should be learned as a means to the end. Focusing on the end goal of this standard requires providing opportunities for students to demonstrate their addition and subtraction skills in a variety of situations, using the identified strategies and discussing the strategies they used.

Learning to read the standards effectively to distinguish the destination (end) from the routes to get there (means) will help teachers make thoughtful, deliberate, and purposeful instructional decisions. A great tactic to use to assess this focus is to ask students why they are doing what they are doing. Their answers should always return back to the end goal of each standard.

Avoiding "Good-Enough" Thinking

A sixth-grade ELA standard for reading literature states:

> Determine the meaning of words and phrases as they are used in a text, including figurative and connotative meanings; analyze the impact of a specific word choice on meaning and tone.

When reviewing this standard, most sixth-grade ELA teachers confirm that they do teach the meaning of words and phrases as they are used in text. Continuing on, they confirm that they do teach figurative and connotative meanings. Typically, though, two-thirds of the way through the standard, their brains reach the "we teach this" point and ignore the rest of the sentence. When prompted to continue, most sixth-grade teachers who read "analyze the impact of a specific word choice on meaning and tone" admit that they really don't spend much, if any, time on this.

The challenge is that understanding how an author's word choice creates tone and meaning, and ultimately determines the quality of the piece of literature, *is* the standard. The use of figurative language, such as, "it was raining cats and dogs," is intended to create a visual or elicit an emotional response such that the reader truly understands the author's meaning. Masterful writers make powerful use of word choice. Edgar Allen Poe's poem, "The Bells" is one example: "Oh the bells, bells, bells, bells, bells, bells, bells; in the clamor and the clanging of the bells." Poe's deliberate choice of repetition creates a foreboding tone and builds the reader's anxiety. It is a much more effective word choice than "the bells rang noisily and incessantly" or "the bells rang repeatedly and loudly." This standard indicates that students should not just offer examples of figurative language, but also understand the power of figurative language to create tone and meaning, providing students with important reading, writing, and speaking skills.

An effective way to accomplish the end goal of this standard might be to provide students, up front, with a scenario that motivates them to learn the strategies. In this case, a teacher might select several powerful examples of this standard in literature and rewrite the texts, using ordinary and less powerful language. The teacher would read both versions aloud to the class and ask students to identify which version offered a more powerful image and evoked greater emotion and why. Once the end goal is in focus, then the teacher can provide individualized, differentiated instructional activities related to figurative language, always returning to the "why" of the activities, which is the end goal.

Consider an eighth-grade geometry standard:

> Understand that a two-dimensional figure is similar to another if the second can be obtained from the first by a sequence of rotations, reflections, translations, and dilations; given two similar two-dimensional figures, describe a sequence that exhibits the similarity between them.

In this case, the end goal is to describe a sequence of rotations, reflections, translations, and dilations that will prove the similarity of two triangles. It is tempting, however, to read the words, "rotations, reflections, translations, and dilations" and assume that the standard is already addressed in the curriculum. Teaching each of these as separate topics will not achieve the standard. Having students identify similar figures in the real world—perhaps found in bridges, architecture, and art—and determine how one figure is rotated, reflected, translated, or dilated to produce the other is the standard. As you can imagine, learning this means engaging in instructional activities that go beyond teacher lessons, note taking, and practice; it means having students engage with the content itself, exploring and describing the natural world around them.

A Tool for Ends–Based Teaching

Once teachers identify the end goal and the strategies and foundational skills for achieving it, they'll need to focus on instruction. How will students learn these strategies and foundational skills? And how will they engage in opportunities to practice the end goal of the standard itself?

Table 2.1 Ends-to-Means-to-End Blank ELA Example

6.RL.4—Determine the meaning of words and phrases as they are used in the text, including figurative and connotative meanings; analyze the impact of a specific word choice on meaning and tone.

My goal is to:	Analyze the impact of a specific word choice on meaning and tone	Learned by:	Modeling of analysis, practice, significant reading, discussion
Which means I must:	Understand the figurative and connotative meanings of words	Learned by:	Instruction, independent learning, practice, reading
Which means I must:	Determine the meaning of words and phrases as they are used in the text	Learned by:	Instruction, independent learning and practice

Table 2.1 offers a strategy for deconstructing a standard and then planning instruction. While this is a planning tool for teachers, it is written from the perspective of the student, and the process should be shared with students so that they understand the end goal at the start of instruction.

Note that the top entry on the left side is the end goal. It may be evident in the standard, or you may have to deduce it from the context. Following that entry are the various strategies and foundational skills that will lead to achievement. Using the phrase, "Which means I must . . ." helps you drill down from the end goal into the strategies and foundational skills. Older students can engage in this process as well to gain a clearer focus on the end goal of instruction. Deconstructing a standard to narrow the instructional focus begins with the end goal and works down to the strategies and foundational skills.

The right side represents how students will *learn* the various strategies and foundational skills and achieve the end goal. Note that learning builds from the bottom up. Once the students have the end goal in focus, they can build all the necessary strategies and foundational skills to accomplish it.

For each entry on the left, identify the type of engagement required to master it. It may be instruction followed by independent practice; it may involve engagement with manipulatives or experiments; it may involve engaging in real-world problems. For this activity, the instructional strategies fall more into broad categories, such as instruction, modeling, practice, engagement with content, etc. Later chapters will broaden the opportunities for learning. Table 2.2 offers another example.

Table 2.2 Ends-to-Means-to-End Blank Math Example

8.G.4—Understand that a two-dimensional figure is similar to another if the second can be obtained from the first by a sequence of rotations, reflections, translations, and dilations; given two similar two-dimensional figures, describe a sequence that exhibits the similarity between them.

My goal is to:	Prove that two figures are similar by describing the sequence of rotations, reflections, translations, and dilations that must be applied to one to have it appear the same as the other	**Learned by:**	Modeling, independent learning, practice, significant engagement with similar figures
Which means I must:	Understand the effect of sequences of rotations, reflections, translations, and dilations	**Learned by:**	Modeling, engagement with rotations, reflections, translations, and dilations
Which means I must:	Define rotations, reflections, translations, and dilations	**Learned by:**	Instruction, independent learning and practice

Your Turn
Getting to Understanding and Application

Turn to the standards for a content area and grade level that are most relevant or of most interest to you. Read through the standards and, in each case, distinguish between the actual end goal and the various strategies or foundational skills that provide a means to the end. The end goal may not always be so obvious; if not, ask yourself what would represent understanding and application. If the strategies are not detailed in the standard, ask yourself what strategies would lead to understanding and application. If it helps, use the graphic model in Figure 2.3 for strategies leading to end goals.

Figure 2.3 Ends-Based Blank Template

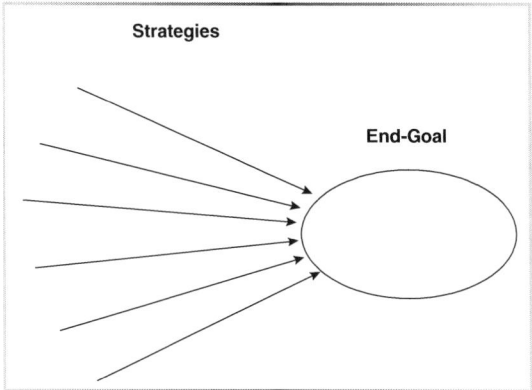

The Big Picture

Each individual standard offers a focused end–means relationship; however, the actual end goal of the skill development in the early grades may not come until subsequent years. The third-grade ELA standard RI.3.3 states:

> Describe the relationship between a series of historical events, scientific ideas or concepts, or steps in technical procedures in a text, using language that pertains to time, sequence, and cause/effect.

Students master the end goal of describing relationships among events, ideas, or concepts; they accomplish this through the use of language that pertains to time, sequence, and cause/effect. However, if you think more about it, what is the point of describing these relationships at all? Sometimes, the actual end goal of the K–12 learning process comes in a later grade level. Eleventh-grade standard RI.11–12.3 states:

> Analyze a complex set of ideas or sequence of events and explain how specific individuals, ideas, or events interact and develop over the course of the text.

The end goal, after all of the learning across the years, is to explain how individuals, ideas, and events develop over the course of the text. This skill goes well beyond learning the sequence and cause-and-effect words of the early years, or the paragraph-based reading comprehension of the intermediate grades, to being able to comprehend an entire text and see how individuals, ideas, and events play out over the course of the text. In order to accomplish that, however, students must master all of those "early grade" skills.

It is, therefore, important to consider a standard, not only in terms of the means–end relationship represented in the standard itself, but also through a look at the standards that build upon the skill in future grades. Progression analysis, covered in chapter 4, will help focus on the end goal at one grade level, the building toward that goal that occurs across the prior years, and the building upon that goal that occurs across the later years.

Your Turn
Using the End to Drive the Means

From the standards you just read, select one and complete the grid in Table 2.3:

1. Enter the standard across the top.

2. Consider the standard and identify the end goal, which will almost always focus on understanding and application. Enter that in the top row on the left.

3. Using a series of "Which means I must . . ." statements, deconstruct the standard into its component parts. You may need to add rows.

4. When the left column is completed, begin at the bottom of the right column and consider how the student will learn this particular concept, skill, or content.

5. Continue to build up to the end goal.

Table 2.3 Ends-to-Means-to-End Blank Template

My goal is to:			Learned by:		
Which means I must:			Learned by:		
Which means I must:			Learned by:		
Which means I must:			Learned by:		
Which means I must:			Learned by:		

The purpose of this activity is to hone in on the essence of the standard and identify the necessary strategies and foundational skills that lead to that end goal. Viewed in this way, the standards are not as daunting to accomplish. As author Ann Voskamp (2011, p. 77) says, "Simplicity is ultimately a matter of focus."

In Summary

Ends-based teaching means:

♦ Carefully reading the standard to determine the end goal, which is almost always related to understanding and application

- Identifying the strategies and foundational skills necessary to achieve the end goal, which are often included in the standard

- Ensuring that instruction begins with a focus on that end goal

- Providing opportunities for students to learn the strategies and foundational skills

- Providing opportunities for students to engage with content in order to build the necessary level of understanding required by the end goal

Chapter 3

The Second Insight

Understanding Requires Grappling

We have the ability to solve almost all of man's grand challenges within the next thirty years.

—Peter Diamandis

The term "grappling," used in the field of martial arts, refers to the twists, turns, and other maneuvers one uses to overcome an opponent. Derived from the noun "grapple," a claw hook used by pirates to seize and hold an enemy ship while preparing to board, it conveys a sense of overcoming. It is, therefore, a powerful word to use to describe the process of solving a challenging problem, as it is used in this text. Envision a student's mind seizing a problem and holding onto it, compelled to solve it.

What does grappling look like? The face of the learner may be intense, with a furrowed brow. The student may ask higher-order questions of himself or herself and others. You may hear comments such as, "maybe if I . . ." followed by "no" as the student self-corrects assumptions. If you interrupt, you may be met with a "wait, wait" as the student is on the verge of a breakthrough in understanding. You will observe moments of excitement accompanied by exclamations and smiles as each level of understanding is reached.

Grappling may be overt and physically observable, as in the case of students working with manipulatives, writing, discussing, conducting a science experiment, building a model, etc. It may also be internal, as in the case of grappling with a concept, word meaning, or content while listening to a speech.

Understanding and Grappling

The CCSS require a level of understanding not typically demanded in schools yet required for success in life after school. The word "understand" means to know how something works and to grasp the meaning of, infer, and comprehend the intended meaning of it. The definition intimates personal, often long-term, experience with the subject. While understanding may involve memorization and definitely involves recall, it requires much more than that of the learner. Achieving understanding involves deconstructing information, making connections to existing knowledge, making and testing predictions, and constructing new meaning—in short, grappling.

The fact that a young child can count to ten and then count from 101 to 110 means he has acquired procedural automaticity (introduced in chapter 1); it does not necessarily mean he understands the value of any single number, nor whether or not it is larger or smaller than another number. The child can memorize the order of numbers but not understand the meaning. Offering two or ten cookies to a young child has no meaning if he does not understand that ten is a larger amount than two.

A student may be able to decode words and read fluently yet still lack understanding of the meaning of those words. "The book is on the table" and "the book is under the table" have very different meanings based on changing one word. Mastering prepositions means more than being able to read them; it means understanding that they establish a relationship between or among objects.

If you understand that the perimeter of an object is the distance around the outer edge, and you understand that in a rectangle, opposite sides are the same measurement, you will be able to derive the formula for the perimeter of a rectangle. If you lack understanding, you will be forced to follow the teacher's procedure, memorize it, and hope to apply it only in situations that mirror the one through which you learned it.

The fact that students forget much of what they learned in prior years speaks to the shortcomings of merely pursuing procedural automaticity. Understanding outfits learners for a lifetime, allowing them to make informed decisions, acquire new knowledge, and apply learning to new situations—"novelty." Understanding ensures that teachers do not have to re-teach topics year after year. The goal of teaching, then, must be understanding, and understanding requires grappling.

You can create an environment that is conducive to grappling through three interdependent strategies: 1) problem-based learning, 2) leveling up (Prensky, 2006), and 3) probing thinking through questioning.

Problem-Based Learning

Problems are natural spurs to learning. Years ago I saw a sixth grader, a struggling reader, come to class with a two-inch thick book, written significantly above his comprehension level, that offered tips for the *Dungeons and Dragons* game he enjoyed playing with his friends. He read sections of that book flawlessly and was totally engrossed in it. If he could read the book, he could learn new strategies to beat his friends. His problem of figuring out how to win spurred him on to build stronger reading skills.

A surfer gets hit with strong and unpredictable waves, tossing her into the water repeatedly. To avoid spending the day *in* the water instead of *on* it, she is spurred on to learn balance and grapples with that skill until she succeeds, thus solving her problem of staying on the board.

Computer game players are presented with obstacles and then work to learn the skills to overcome them. People who travel to a foreign country are motivated to learn key phrases in order to find their way around and get what they need. A brain surgeon is faced with an unusually challenging tumor and sets out to research the latest surgical methods. Problems motivate! When faced with an open-ended problem, there is a need to overcome the challenge of the unknown answer. The problem-solver will make attempts, consider feedback, build new skills, all in search of a plausible answer; this is the process of grappling.

Getting students grappling with authentic, open-ended problems will prepare them for the demands of the CCSS, particularly given that many of the standards include solving real-world problems. The world needs problem-finders, innovators, and entrepreneurs. As Peter Diamandis, founder of the Xprize Foundation, says, "We have the ability to solve almost all of man's grand challenges within the next thirty years."

Use Open-Ended Problems

Through grappling, the problem-solver builds understanding. Projects that are closed-ended may be interesting and fun; however, they tend to require only procedural learning. Drawing a map of a region of the world is a project that requires procedural knowledge; designing a two-week tour of the region that offers a great number of experiences in a short period of time is a problem that requires novelty, which requires understanding, and thus, grappling. In the latter problem-based scenario, the student will still use procedural knowledge to draw a map, but build greater understanding of the region through deciding the best routes to use to accomplish the task.

Using a kit and following directions to build a CO_2 car is a project that requires procedural learning; designing an original CO_2 car to compete on a particular track is a problem that requires novelty, which requires understanding, and thus, grappling. In the latter case, the student may still begin by designing a car from a kit, but then question each component and grapple with how to make the car more efficient and faster.

Asking students to draw three pictures representing the sequence of a story requires procedural knowledge of sequencing; asking them to draw three picture representing the sequence of what could happen next requires novelty, which requires understanding, and thus, grappling. Again, developing the original sequence requires first sequencing the actual events of the story, but it also requires an understanding of characters, setting, and plot to grapple with what a "what next" scenario might be that is consistent with the story.

Writing an original fairy tale requires a student to grapple with the elements of a fairy tale. Identifying a possible new element on the periodic table requires a student to grapple with the structure and meaning of the periodic table. Developing a full complement of exercises to improve the physical fitness of a person requires a student to grapple with the structure and function of the organs and muscles of the human body, and the types of exercises that address the health of each. Designing a polyhedral lighting fixture for an eccentric mathematician requires grappling with three-dimensional, and thus two-dimensional, geometry and measurement. Writing music to accompany an ad for a favorite product requires the student to grapple with the concepts and skills related to chords, notes, tempo, and more. The open-ended nature of the problem promotes grappling over mere information retrieval and reporting.

Use Compelling Problems

Grappling with academic problems presumes the problems are worthy of the grappling process. They must be challenging, without obvious answers, not Google-able; they must be compelling, piquing the interest of the students. The more authentic and open-ended the problem, the more compelling it is. Asking students to write an essay about the Declaration of Independence and how the U.S. became an independent country is not compelling. Asking them to create a web page or printed guide for future citizens is more compelling, as it adds an authentic audience. In a world of Internet access and reality television, asking students to consider territories in the world still under colonial rule today and offer up a plan for their quest for independence, based on lessons learned from the U.S. experience, can be even more compelling. This last problem challenges students to tackle a real-world problem yet unsolved in the world today; students tend to like such challenges.

In the case of the tasks just presented, the first (the essay) simply requires the student to locate information and feed it back. Avoid this type of task as the overarching problem, as it focuses more on the ability to locate and present information than on the meaning of content itself. The second task (the future citizens' website) requires students to locate information and feed it back with a specific audience in mind. This is somewhat better; however, the student will be focusing more on language and presentation than the content of social studies. The third task (solving a world problem) requires students to delve into the content and apply it to a new situation. This is the type of problem appearing more and more on standardized tests. This type of problem requires an "understanding" of the content in order to apply it. If students understand that the colonists were angry that they were paying taxes on tea to England, feeling the taxes were not benefitting the colonies, they can consider the types of revenue being paid by a current territory to its mother country to determine what avenues the people might consider to challenge the taxation. If students merely create timelines and memorize events without gaining understanding, they will be hard-pressed to apply the learning to another situation.

Asking fourth-grade students to create a poster of the food plate to hang in the halls is fun and requires them to learn about nutrition. Asking them to analyze the school lunch program to make recommendations to the food services director is compelling; they will need to apply learning to a real-world situation. A teacher whose class tackled this problem ended up convincing the food services director to add snap peas and strawberry shortcake to the lunch menu. Asking high-school students to solve word problems using statistics addresses content; asking them to calculate the power of a local company's social network and offer scenarios for how they can increase that power is compelling. Students are faced with a real-world problem, an audience, a topic with which they are personally familiar, and the chance to make a difference. A compelling problem will cause a student to focus, locate existing information, consider cause-and-effect relationships, analyze, synthesize—grapple!

Present the Problem Up Front

Most classroom instruction begins with lower-order foundational skills and basic concepts that build to more complex skills and concepts. Toward the end of the unit, students are then presented with a culminating project through which to apply the skills. A math teacher might teach ratio, then proportion, then how to solve proportion problems, before asking students to create a scale drawing of the classroom, and before asking them to redesign the classroom. However, during times of key instruction, the student has no felt need to learn the skill; upon being presented with the culminating activity, the student is challenged to remember what was taught. Alternatively, when the problem is presented up front, students have a felt need to pay attention to the teacher's instruction and to engage meaningfully in learning activities, as each relates to the final product.

The intent of presenting the problem up front is to motivate students to learn and, more importantly, retain learning. Presenting subject-area content within a greater context increases the likelihood of long-term retention. Consider the scenarios that follow.

Scenario 1: "You are going to redesign the classroom to be more student friendly, more conducive to learning. Create a scale drawing of the classroom and furniture, rearranging the furniture to create a better learning environment. The class will then vote on the designs to try, selecting one each month."

Scenario 2: "Our town has many community helpers to keep us safe and help us in our daily lives. They work very hard and have to overcome many obstacles. How can we make their work easier? You are going to create a guide called 'Helping Them Help Us' that shows how we can help community service providers perform their duties."

Scenario 3: "Scientists have discovered single-celled organisms that can clean radioactive water by ingesting radioactive water and excreting an inert substance. Could they be the answer to cleaning up radioactive water that results from nuclear power plants? Delve into the metabolism of single-celled organisms and make your case."

These three problem-based scenarios are the introductions to units of study in math, social studies, and science, respectively. When presented at the start of a unit, as opposed to being used as culminating activities, they challenge students to solve problems that they yet don't know how to solve, thus driving them into the curriculum for answers. A well-crafted problem sets the stage for students to grapple with content to build understanding and apply it to the problem situation. Scenario 1 causes students to grapple with solving proportion problems in order to scale down their measurements. Scenario 2 causes students to grapple with the challenges faced by community workers, such as the challenge of firefighters knowing how many people and pets are in a burning house, in order to present suggestions for how people can help them perform their jobs better or more easily. Scenario 3 causes students to grapple with the metabolism of single-celled organisms to determine how they could ingest radioactive material and excrete non-radioactive material. A well-crafted problem should be content focused.

Each scenario challenges students to solve a problem that teachers intend to be motivating. In Scenario 1, middle-school students have the opportunity to redesign the classroom to their own unique plan. In Scenario 2, young students have the opportunity to help the local police, postal worker, crossing guard, firefighters, and others perform their jobs more easily. In Scenario 3, middle- or high-school students have the opportunity to offer a solution to a yet-unsolved global problem. The motivation may come from the topic itself, if it is of particular interest to students; it may come from the challenge itself and the love of a good problem; it may come from a sense of competition; it may come from a feeling of independence and the ability to take charge of their own learning. Procedural automaticity does not require motivation, only compliance; grappling requires motivation and engagement.

How can students solve the problem when they don't know the content? They can't! If they could, there'd be no point in offering the problem as a context for building new understandings. The purpose of presenting the problem at the start of the unit is to motivate students and create the conditions under which information will be stored in long-term memory. Babies can't talk, but they are motivated to learn because they hear others talking. We wouldn't consider being silent in the presence of a child until that child learns to talk; why should we consider withholding challenges until students can address them?

Once students have the goal in sight, the teacher provides students with opportunities to learn the content. It is through a collection of rich and diverse learning activities—all of which allow each student to be increasingly challenged above his or her ability level—that students build understanding. Teachers can't stop with the problem; they must then provide the means to achieve the goal. As the architect of a powerful learning environment, the teacher designs learning activities to address various cognitive levels and learning modalities, providing a differentiated environment through which students can access learning toward solving the problem. Students will also seek out opportunities to learn, knowing that they need the content to solve the problem.

Leveling Up

The typical student, at any age level, has a seemingly inordinate attention span for computer and video games. Marc Prensky (2006) attributes this to a technique used by game developers known as "leveling up." You may have heard of the game app (a computer application designed to run on mobile devices) called *Candy Crush Saga* (www.candycrushsaga.com).

At first, the premise seems simple enough. You have a grid of six colored candies. You move a candy up, down, or across to complete a row of three, at which point they are crushed and other candies fall into their places. At first, your goal is to collect a certain number of points, which, once achieved, advances you to the next level. Soon you realize that if you align four candies instead of just three, you have a powerful new candy that can clear an entire row, so you set your sights on creating groups of fours. You then realize that if you create groupings of five, you have an even more powerful candy; and if you combine power candies, you can more easily crush an entire board. Each level introduces a new challenge and requires a specific strategy. Sometimes you have to navigate ingredients from the top to the bottom of the screen by crushing the candies in the ingredient's path; other times you have to collect a designated number of points within a time limit or a designated number of moves. The game requires constant higher-order thinking. It's a CCSS playground! You search for patterns, build strategies, consider the cause-and-effect aspect of specific moves, ward off candy invaders that will thwart your progress, and communicate with others to gain lives. At each new level, the player becomes a problem-finder, working quickly to figure out what challenges lay ahead at this level.

Each level prepares you for the next. Once you build skill in identifying how to create groupings of four or five candies, chocolates appear and cover your candy, making it more difficult for you to achieve your goal. As you build your skills in achieving the goal while staving off the creeping chocolates, bombs appear that must be disarmed in a number of moves. At the time of this writing, the makers of *Candy Crush Saga* had created over a thousand levels for the happy gamer to tackle. It is a wonderful example of leveling up on the part of the game designers and of the cognitive progression that takes place as you succeed at each level: from simply aligning candies, to aligning candies under the pressure of time or moves, to doing so while eliminating chocolates and bombs, to who knows what? The type of learning required to succeed at a level is procedural automaticity, and after several or many tries at a level, you will succeed. The type of learning required to devise a strategy at a new level is novelty.

The game player's confidence that he or she can meet each new challenge provides the impetus to continue playing, level after level, as long as each new level is not too easy or too hard. Prensky relates this to the concept of being in "flow" (Csikszentmilhalyi, 1990)—when you are so engrossed in an activity that you lose track of time and surrounding events. Prensky posits that in game playing, students are in flow when the challenges with which they are presented are just above their ability level (see Figure 3.1). If the challenge of the situation is much lower than the students' capabilities,

Figure 3.1   Flow by Csikszentmilhalyi

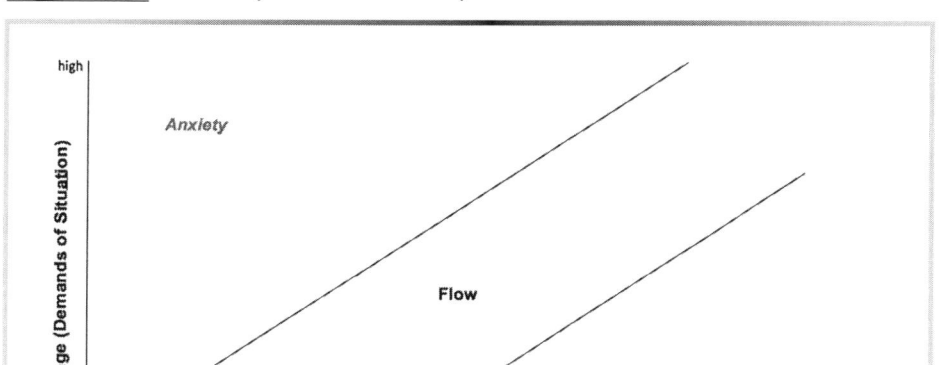

they will most likely become bored and disengage; conversely, if the challenge is much higher than the students' capabilities, they will become anxious and disengage. By leveling up the instructional activities presented to students, the teacher can ensure the students will remain engaged in a state of grappling to build understanding.

While the content-focused, problem-based scenario should be in and of itself reasonably challenging, the tasks and learning activities along the way should provide students with that leveling-up experience to foster grappling to build understanding. This speaks to the need for differentiation, given that not all students will come to the problem with the same ability level.

Students who are working to write an original myth will need to learn the characteristics of a myth and certain writing techniques to create more powerful imagery. While all students in a class may be faced with writing a myth, the readiness of each to learn—for example, using metaphors, building a plot line, and developing mythological characters—will vary from student to student. Providing activities for each skill that allow students to be grappling at a level just above their individual ability level will ensure that each student's momentum for learning builds as the unit progresses.

Throughout a problem-based learning unit, the teacher can foster grappling through leveling up by offering a variety of learning opportunities, including the more hands-on/minds-on experiences of manipulatives, learning centers, simulations, and computer apps. The following sections explore these experiences in more detail.

Manipulatives

Cuisenaire rods were first invented by a Belgian teacher, George Cuisenaire, in 1931; but they were popularized by Caleb Gattegno (founder of the Association of Teachers of Mathematics), who saw them as instrumental in building math concepts and skills: Give students a collection of various-sized colored rods and let them explore. The rods are different sizes; each size has a corresponding color. The rods can be lined up to represent increasing quantities. A white rod is the smallest quantity, a single unit; some rods are double the size of others. The rods can be combined to create squares. They can be stacked to create cubes. As students explore with the rods, they generate questions and ideas, pursue them, and build understandings. Each understanding leads to another question: Can every rod be represented by a number of the white rods, the single unit? Why do the rods stop at a certain length? What length is that? Does a length of ten have special meaning? Can I create a pattern of rods that forms a rectangular prism? And so forth.

Cuisenaire rods, geometric shapes, fraction pieces, letter and sound blocks, tessellations, molecule parts, word tiles, music tiles, and other manipulatives allow students to use concrete experiences to form abstract understandings. No student is ever too old for manipulatives! Students across the grade levels should be given opportunities to make sense of difficult concepts through manipulatives. Just gather hands-on components that can be manipulated into different configurations to create new items, allowing students to grapple with content and build understanding. Manipulatives promote a natural leveling up as students tend to tackle challenges that are at an appropriate level, which then generate ideas for higher levels of thinking.

Learning Centers

Similar to manipulatives, learning centers can be designed to offer hands-on experiences that foster grappling that leads to understanding. A microscope with slides of various organisms allows students to explore, question, and pose hypotheses to be tested. A learning center with pictures and words to be matched can build awareness of patterns related to sounds and the letters that produce them. An artist's learning center can provide opportunities to explore how colors mix into other colors. A construction learning center can build physics concepts and a greater understanding of simple machines. A music learning center can cause students to grapple with how a combination of notes can create a tune and how notes relate to one another. An oil spill learning center can allow environmental science students to explore effective ways of extracting oil from water.

Simulations

Simulated environments allow students to interact with real-world concepts, such as revolutionary war, space exploration, genetics, communicating in a foreign country, starting a business, flight, mixing chemicals, colonization, and more. In pre-school and kindergarten, students engage in simulations through play: grocery store, cooking, construction, theater, and more. Through the grade levels, computer programs and online simulations offer students opportunities to explore real-world situations from the classroom. A simulation offers a chain of cause-and-effect relationships. The player takes an action and, based on that action, receives information on the result of that action. Throughout a simulation, students grapple with content to develop possible actions; they engage in convergent thinking to analyze the cause of the action. Simulations allow students to engage in scenarios that otherwise would be impossible in the classroom, providing a powerful venue for grappling with content to build understanding and to apply learning.

Computer Apps

Java applets first made it possible for students to manipulate objects easily on screen, with students of math and science benefiting the most. Using Java applets, students can use a computer to manipulate fraction pieces, tessellations, and polyhedra; balance equations; explore physics concepts; and more. With the advent of the iPad and other tablet and smart phone devices, students can manipulate on-screen objects with their fingers, increasing the power of technology to engage them in myriad learning opportunities. Apps provide students with on-screen manipulatives and simulations that can promote grappling with content.

Probing Thinking Through Questions

The third strategy to ensure a classroom culture of grappling is the interaction between student and teacher. Problem solving promotes both divergent thinking (questioning, brainstorming) and convergent thinking (solution finding, testing, evaluation). Both divergent and convergent thinking are present in the grappling process, and both should be deliberately facilitated by the teacher. While it may appear that students are engaged and even engrossed in the problem, it would be detrimental to the learning process for the teacher to simply leave them to work on their own and only respond to questions posed by students. Students don't know what they don't know; teachers probe student thinking and trigger "aha" experiences through their questioning.

Caleb Gattegno (1987) presented the theory of the subordination of teaching to learning. He suggested that teachers present a problem and then observe students engaging with it, seeking to identify how their thought processes are progressing. At an appropriate time, the teacher asks questions that probe students' thinking, thus promoting grappling.

If you notice the students building the CO_2 car putting weight on the back of the car, you might first ask why they chose to do this, and then ask how they think weight will positively affect speed. Is there a point at which the weight will negatively affect speed? You might ask students designing a tour of an area of the country how they know their route is the most efficient for seeing all of the stops using the shortest amount of travel time. If they simply selected the shortest route, you might ask them how speed limits or numbers of lanes on the roads might affect their arrival time at the next stop on the tour. You might ask story writers how they would feel if they were in the character's place, and then what words they used or could use to convey those feelings. Through teachers' questioning (addressed more fully in chapter 8), students' minds will open to further possibilities; they will stop and think through why they made the decisions they did; and they will either justify their decisions or consider new ones. A good question does not end with an answer; it causes students to self-reflect and produce more questions.

Masterful teachers ask questions that promote both divergent and convergent thinking, increasing the probability that students will engage in grappling with content to construct meaning. As an example, to spark divergent and convergent thinking, have any grade level of students work in teams of three or four, and give them a collection of straws, tape, and paper clips. Ask them to create the tallest freestanding structure they can; then watch their actions and listen to their questions and comments. You will gain insights into their thinking processes as you do. You can then begin to ask questions: Have them explain why they took a particular step; what they think will contribute to designing the largest freestanding structure; how they arrived at various decisions; and so forth. You can pose alternative solutions, such as, "What do you think would happen if you taped straws end-to-end to make one long straw?" While you may know the answer, it's important not to lead students to your answer, but rather to ask questions that will prompt them to explore the concepts underlying the answer.

Questions that promote divergent thinking tend to be very open-ended, such as:

- ♦ Suppose . . . ?
- ♦ What if . . . ?
- ♦ Can you predict . . . ?
- ♦ What are the implications . . . ?
- ♦ How many ways . . . ?
- ♦ What is another way to look at . . . ?
- ♦ What options exist for . . . ?

Questions that promote convergent thinking tend to focus on a correct answer or the ability to defend an answer, such as:

- ♦ Why did this happen?
- ♦ How does this work?
- ♦ In what ways . . . ?
- ♦ What evidence do you have . . . ?
- ♦ Can you explain . . . ?
- ♦ How often . . . ?
- ♦ What is the outcome . . . ?

Questions are a powerful way to promote grappling through divergent and convergent thinking. For any given unit of study, consider the key concepts and skills you expect students to learn. Then brainstorm the questions you might ask to prompt divergent and convergent thinking. Begin with broader open-ended questions to allow students to mentally work their way to the details. Encourage students to ask themselves questions that will lead to greater understanding. Simply asking, "What are you thinking about?" can accomplish this. When you ask students a convergent question, such as "Why did this happen?" follow it with a divergent question, such as, "What if . . .?"

The Common Core State Standards and Grappling

The CCSS lay out clear expectations for students to apply learning, with many standards stating that students will "solve real-world problems." Newer standardized tests present students with application challenges. Successful application of knowledge in problem-solving situations is the true test of understanding. The three interdependent strategies of using problem-based learning, leveling up, and probing thinking through questioning will lead students to success in CCSS achievement.

As an example, second graders who are writing their own fairy tales to offer a history, moral, or cautionary advice about being in second grade (problem-based learning) will address the following CCSS writing standard:

> Write narratives in which they recount a well-elaborated event or short sequence of events, include details to describe actions, thoughts, and feelings, use temporal words to signal event order, and provide a sense of closure.

To accomplish this task, they will have to read fairy tales and build skills through differentiated activities suited to their ability level (leveling up). They will address the following two related standards:

> Recount stories, including fables and folktales from diverse cultures, and determine their central message, lesson, or moral.

> Describe how characters in a story respond to major events and challenges.

While the entire unit may take four weeks, students will engage in smaller challenges throughout the unit: Decide how a character in a fairy tale might respond to a particular event; determine how to describe a character well for your own story; build a word wall of temporal words to use in your story; and so forth. The motivation to write an original fairy tale about second grade will drive a felt need to learn a variety of skills and concepts, for which the teacher must determine appropriate learning activities to fuel success. Leveling up the skill of character development might include activities and graphic organizers that begin with simply a name, gender, age, and look; next, the student might consider what magic power the character has; and then the student might describe the character's personality and relationships with other characters. While students are working, well-placed and well-crafted questions by the teacher will fuel learning through grappling.

As another example, students who are exploring the extent to which single-celled organisms can be used to clean up radioactive water will address the following ELA standards for science and technical subjects:

> Integrate and evaluate multiple sources of information presented in diverse formats and media (e.g., quantitative data, video, multimedia) in order to address a question or solve a problem.

To accomplish this, they will need to engage in activities that provide a leveling up related to reading and comprehending scientific texts, such as:

> Determine the meaning of symbols, key terms, and other domain-specific words and phrases as they are used in a specific scientific or technical context. . . .

They will also address this standard:

> Follow precisely a complex multistep procedure when carrying out experiments, taking measurements, or performing technical tasks; analyze the specific results based on explanations in the text.

Again, a leveling up would provide students with opportunities to carry out increasingly complex experiments, taking increasingly complex measurements. As students research the topic through informational text, they might analyze primary cause-and-effect relationships (such as single-celled organisms convert radioactive material to inert material), then secondary cause-and-effect relationships (which means the clean water is able to support plant life), and then tertiary cause-and-effect relationships (which means plant life increases the oxygenation of the water). Teachers' probing questions would cause students to delve more deeply into the content.

Building the level of understanding required of the CCSS through grappling will cause a shift in the role of the teacher. Instead of focusing on presentations, which often have to be tailored to address the average student, the teacher will engage in rich dialogue with students, providing a scaffold for struggling students, and pushing advanced students to higher levels of thinking. Together, problem-based learning, leveling up, and probing questions will create a classroom culture of grappling toward understanding.

Your Turn . . .

Identify a unit of study of interest to you. Brainstorm a possible authentic, open-ended problem students could tackle that would require the unit content.

Select one skill or concept from the unit. Brainstorm three activities that level up in sophistication to build toward mastery.

Using that same skill or concept, generate some divergent thinking questions and some convergent thinking questions that could help students build a deeper understanding.

In Summary

Grappling toward understanding means:

♦ Using authentic, open-ended problems presented up front to create a motivation and context for learning

♦ Developing learning activities that allow for leveling up to ensure students are tackling challenges just above their ability level to keep them engaged

♦ Using manipulatives, learning centers, simulations, and computer apps to provide leveling-up activities that cause students to grapple

♦ Asking probing questions that promote both divergent and convergent thinking

Chapter 4

The Third Insight

Cognitive Progression Is a Lever for Achievement

Give me a lever long enough . . . and I shall move the world.

—Archimedes

Cognition, simply put, is another word for thinking. Specifically, cognitive skills are those mental processes that use thought, experience, and the senses to construct meaning. You learned to write simple sentences years ago, such as, "The dog barked." Having mastered that, you probably learned to create compound sentences, such as, "The dog barked and ran around." Next, you would have been ready to master complex sentences, such as, "The dog barked and the cat ran under the couch." At each level, your brain tucked away new learning and was ready to take on the next learning challenge. The continued building upon learning to achieve at increasingly higher levels is cognitive progression.

Human beings love to learn; they only grow weary of learning when the learning challenges are too hard or too easy. As teachers consider their curriculum, they can deliberately plan instruction to "level up," as introduced in chapter 3, taking into account how the brain builds upon prior learning to tackle new learning. That is, teachers can leverage cognitive progression to raise student achievement. There is no limit to what students can learn, once engaged in a purposeful process of cognitive progression.

Cognitive Progression and the Standards

Consider the following word problems and the number of calculations and thought processes that would be required for each:

1. Jamal bought $45 worth of groceries. Sales tax is 7%. How much did Jamal have to pay in sales tax?

2. Jamal bought $45 worth of groceries. Sales tax is 7%. What was Jamal's total bill?

3. Jamal bought $45 worth of groceries, of which $28 were taxable. Sales tax is 7%. What was Jamal's total bill?

4. Jamal bought $45 worth of groceries, of which $17 were not taxable. Sales tax is 7%. What was Jamal's total bill?

5. Jamal bought $45 worth of groceries, of which $17 were not taxable. Sales tax is 7%. If Jamal drove ten miles to the next county, the sales tax would be 3/8% less than his home county. How much would he save if he purchased his groceries in the next county?

All word problems are not alike! Solving problem "a" requires a basic skill: calculating sales tax. Solving problem "b" requires two basic skills: calculating the sales tax and then adding it to the subtotal. Solving problem "c" requires similar skills but also the ability to understand applying tax to only a portion of the bill. Solving problem "d" requires an understanding of how to determine the taxable portion and then multiple steps of subtracting, multiplying, and adding. The student must realize that if $17 of the groceries are not taxable, the first step is to identify the price of the groceries that were taxable, requiring subtraction before computing the sales tax and total bill. Solving problem "e" requires fraction-to-decimal conversion on top of the other skills, with the added requirement of making a comparison. Progressively more complex thinking depends upon a strong level of understanding at each level. Understanding is at the heart of the CCSS.

Consider the following standards and what progression of steps might be used to ensure that students can achieve the level of understanding required.

Solve two-step word problems using the four operations. Represent these problems using equations with a letter standing for the unknown quantity. Assess the reasonableness of answers using mental computation and estimation strategies including rounding.

The above third-grade math standard for operations and algebraic thinking requires the use of several skills and strategies at once. To build toward this standard, first, students would need to master solving one-step word problems using each of the four operations. Then they would need to use mental computation and estimation to check for reasonableness. Then they would need to solve similar problems using variables. Finally, they would need to apply all these skills in solving two-step problems.

> Solve real-world and mathematical problems by graphing points in all four quadrants of the coordinate plane. Include use of coordinates and absolute value to find distances between points with the same first coordinate or the same second coordinate.

The above sixth-grade standard requires an understanding of the coordinate plane and its use in solving problems, as well as absolute value. The progression here begins with plotting points on the coordinate plane, writing equations to represent problems, generating sets of coordinate points for an equation, and so forth.

> Gather relevant information from multiple print and digital sources, using search terms effectively; assess the credibility and accuracy of each source; and quote or paraphrase the data and conclusions of others while avoiding plagiarism and following a standard format for citation.

While the above eighth-grade standard is from the ELA standards, the level of understanding and thinking required to achieve it is evident. It's not enough to find information; the student has to determine its credibility and be able to paraphrase, if not quote, to avoid plagiarism, using a standard citation. At one glance, this seems like a lot to accomplish. Break it down into smaller pieces and build toward the standard, and beyond, and students will gain the level of understanding needed for the CCSS.

> Evaluate authors' differing points of view on the same historical event or issue by assessing the authors' claims, reasoning, and evidence.

In this high-school standard for literacy in history/social studies, the student needs to be able to understand multiple authors' accounts of the same historical event or issue; assess each author's account through the claims made, reasoning, and evidence offered; and evaluate them. This standard is packed with higher-order thinking that is best addressed through cognitive progression.

Basic skills can be mastered through rote memorization and procedural automaticity; beyond the basic skills lies a world of analysis, synthesis, and evaluation—"novelty." These are the goals of the CCSS; and they are achieved not through curriculum and syllabi alone, but through careful attention to cognitive progression.

The Cognitive Word Wall

Let's take a deeper look at the brain's thinking processes. A common cognitive exercise (Sweller, 1999) is to flash a group of the following letters in front of the viewer and allow three seconds to commit them to memory:

WO UIB MES LUS A

Most people cannot remember all of the letters in three seconds. That's because the human brain can only hold about seven pieces of information in working memory at one time (Miller, 1956), and the above list includes twelve pieces of information. The next step in the exercise is to show the same letters divided differently:

WOU IBM ESL USA

Most people can remember all of the letters presented this way. That's because the letters are chunked into meaningful groupings and thus represent only four pieces of information. The human brain, for example, treats the name of the company IBM as one piece of information, not three. WOU is recognized as the beginning of the word would; ESL is a common acronym for educators; and USA is also easily recognizable as a meaningful collection of letters. An organized collection of information based on some pattern or meaningful connection is a *schema*. In this case, each of the letter clusters is a schema.

Young students build knowledge of each of the letters of the alphabet. Next, they group letters into meaningful clusters and learn sight words, such as these: the, ball, and, foot, etc. These are now schemas (or schemata) added to their knowledge bank. They can build new schemas by combining existing ones, such as discovering the word "football" as the combination of "foot" and "ball." The brain continuously builds upon schemas to increase knowledge.

As the brain encounters information, it must perform a series of cognitive processes—those responsible for obtaining, making sense of, and storing knowledge. For example, you see someone wave as the person approaches you and says a word you don't understand: *hola*. First, you must attend to the situation; attention is a cognitive process. Then you perceive a wave and a sound; perception is a cognitive process. You will use the cognitive process of representation to identify the wave of a person walking toward you as a friendly greeting. Most likely, you will use the cognitive process of reasoning to determine that *hola* is a greeting, perhaps hello. That's a simplistic breakdown, as you will, in actuality, use dozens of cognitive processes to navigate the situation and learn the new word. Table 4.1 offers a partial list of the more common cognitive processes. While this is not intended to be a textbook of cognitive science, it is important to realize the level of brain activity that goes into making sense of the simplest piece of content presented by a teacher.

Given that all pieces of information must be processed, the brain is continually taking action in the pursuit of learning. Consider the examples of letters presented at the start of this section. Processing the letter combinations required attention, perception, apperception, representation, discrimination, categorization, and memorization. However, in the case of

Table 4.1 Cognitive Processes

Cognitive Process	Definition (The process of . . .)
Acquisition	Adding a skill or knowledge to one's mental storehouse
Analysis	Separating information into component parts and examining the interrelationships
Apperception	Relating newly identified qualities of an object to past experience
Attention	Concentrating on one piece of information
Awareness	Having knowledge of something
Believing	Developing convictions
Categorization	Sorting information by like characteristics
Discrimination	Distinguishing two or more pieces of information from one another based on unlike characteristics
Intuition	Knowing instinctively
Justification	Demonstrating or proving something to be correct or valid
Memorization	Committing to memory
Perception	Becoming aware through the senses, particularly sight or hearing
Reasoning	Drawing conclusions from facts or evidence
Representation	Identifying one piece of information as standing for another
Synthesis	Combining elements to create a new whole

the first group of letters, the brain had to process each letter independently, attempting to make connections among the letters in each grouping. In the second case, the brain processed meaningful groupings of letters with which it was already familiar, such as, "USA." The degree to which working memory must perform processes to gain understanding is referred to as *cognitive load*. In the opening exercise, the list "WO UIB MES LUS A" had a cognitive load of 12; the list "WOU IBM ESL USA" had a cognitive load of 4, because the letters were arranged into more meaningful groupings. When presenting new information to students, the lower the cognitive load, the better.

As another example, the name of this section is a play on words. When you read "Cognitive Word Wall," you first had to process at least two pieces of information, the words or phrases themselves. If you are an educator you may already have a schema for "word wall," visualizing a classroom word wall. To solidify understanding by creating context, your thoughts may then have gone to the classroom and to the thought that this chapter was going to tell you how to make something called a cognitive word wall for students. You may have had to spend more brain power processing the word "cognitive" if it wasn't in your everyday vocabulary. Your brain had to then process even more as you read, to determine that this was a section on vocabulary words for you, not something you would create for students. This section title brings with it a good amount of cognitive load. If it were called "Cognitive Science Vocabulary," your brain would have understood the content of the section more quickly. (Sorry about that, but I wanted to offer an illustrative example.)

John Sweller (1988) developed Cognitive Load Theory, which emphasizes the need for strategic development of learning activities to reduce cognitive load and increase the likelihood of learning. Wikipedia offers a good example: imagine studying a subject area in a foreign language as opposed to your native language. The former situation requires you to not only make sense of the subject but to navigate the non-native language, thus carrying a higher cognitive load than the latter situation of studying in your native language. The goal of effective instruction is to provide students with experiences that require low cognitive load to build new schemas, continually building toward greater understanding and knowledge acquisition.

Using Cognitive Progression in Lesson Design

Consider a curricular objective of interest to you as we work through the example of teaching students about adjectives. As you read about the related cognitive progression, decide how this would apply to your curriculum objective.

Adjectives modify nouns. The first question you have to ask yourself is, "Do all of my students know what a noun is?" For some students, you may need to provide concrete examples of nouns in a learning center and ask them to describe these items. Your intent is to solidify the concept of nouns, while introducing the concept of adjectives. For others, begin with a learning activity that introduces the concept or skill at the lowest level. In this case, you might have students brainstorm descriptive words that are very obvious. Have them describe the color, the number of items, and other visual characteristics. Then have the students describe items based on the other senses: have them touch items and describe how they feel, have them listen and describe what they hear, have them smell items and describe the scent. This is a higher cognitive level than simply taking in colors and numbers. So far, they are describing only very concrete "things"; but nouns also represent persons and places. Have students brainstorm words to describe people they know, being careful not to describe a "thing" about the person. For example, tall would be acceptable, but in the case of brown hair, "brown" describes "hair." They will most likely move beyond the visual to include adjectives such as funny, smart, pretty, etc. Describing places will require slightly more abstract thinking because students have to visualize a place and may not be as familiar with them as they are with the people they know. They may brainstorm phrases like sunny Florida, crowded playground, busy airport, noisy restaurant, etc. After this initial level of exploration, have students brainstorm a definition for "adjective" and work with them to develop that definition. Now they have to abstract from their experiences a definition.

While it is not important for students to master certain applications of adjectives before others, if teachers explore how cognition builds upon cognition to achieve increasingly higher levels of thinking, they will be able to leverage cognitive progression to accelerate academic achievement. Defining an adjective as a word that describes a noun, and then asking students to brainstorm words, would be overwhelming to some, or many, students. Building from simple descriptions of things they can see and hold to persons and places creates that powerful "leveling up" described in chapter 3.

Continue to increase the use of cognitive skills related to learning about adjectives by introducing the idea that adjectives answer one of four questions: how many?, what kind?, which one, and whose? Students have already answered the "how many?" and "what kind?" questions, so next tackle the "whose?" adjectives, such as "Juan's desk," "Brielle's pencil," etc. This requires students to consider ownership. Moving to a higher cognitive level, provide students with multiple items and ask them how they can designate which one they are choosing. For example, answers to a "which one?" question might be "the blue shirt," "the green shirt," and "the yellow shirt." Have students describe what sets one apart from the other, and how they could identify one shirt over the others; this task involves comparing and contrasting items—a higher cognitive skill than merely describing color, for example. Next, move to strings of adjectives, such as, "the big, furry, red cat." Students must ensure that each word directly describes the noun. In the phrase, "the very big, furry, red cat," the word "very" is not an adjective. (For more advanced students, you can introduce the concept of an adverb as describing an adjective.)

Next, you might consider having students search for better adjectives, more specific words. A special education teacher created a graduated word wall that encouraged students to list an adjective and then come up with a better and perhaps even better word in terms of how descriptive it is. For example, a "big book" could mean that it covers a large surface area or that it weighs a lot. The latter might better be described as a "hefty book" while the former might better be described as an "oversized book." Since a "big man" could mean tall or heavy, the man could be even better described as towering or hefty, respectively. Having students search for synonyms will require them to think through specific meanings of words and how some adjectives are more descriptive than others, taking into account misconceptions if they use adjectives that are too vague. Obviously, this activity would require a much higher cognitive level than merely describing nouns.

Table 4.2 offers the cognitive progression of learning adjectives as detailed in the preceding paragraphs. Using this method, you can deconstruct any skill or concept to consider how the mind would most likely tackle it. If instruction is then matched to increasing cognitive levels, students will be more likely to build confidence and remain engaged in learning.

Table 4.2 Cognitive Progression Example

Describe obvious visual characteristics of items: color, size, number of items, etc.
Describe items based on senses other than sight.
Describe people.
Describe places.
Develop a working definition for adjectives.
Consider the four questions adjectives answer.
Explore adjectives that answer the question, "whose?"
Explore adjectives that answer the question, "which one?"
Brainstorm strings of adjectives to describe one noun.
Brainstorm synonyms that would more specifically describe an aspect of a noun.

Third Insight: Cognitive Progression

As Archimedes said, "Give me a lever long enough . . . and I shall move the world." Cognitive progression provides teachers with the lever to move the minds of their students.

Cognitive Progression Across the Grade Levels in the ELA Standards

While the previous discussion focused on the cognitive progression for learning a skill or concept, the CCSS also rely on cognitive progression across the grade levels. Teachers should consider the standards in the grades that come before and after theirs, where applicable. This will help them to ensure that they are designing for purposeful instruction targeted to grade level expectations or above so that they prepare students within the larger context of learning across the grade levels. Each of the ELA strands includes a set of standards that progress from grade level to grade level. For example, consider the writing standard for opinion/argumentative writing. In kindergarten, the standard reads:

> Use a combination of drawing, dictating, and writing to compose opinion pieces in which they tell a reader the topic or the name of the book they are writing about and state an opinion or preference about the topic or book (e.g., My favorite book is . . .).

In first grade, the standard reads:

> Write opinion pieces in which they introduce the topic or name the book they are writing about, state an opinion, supply a reason for the opinion, and provide some sense of closure.

In second grade, the standard reads:

> Write opinion pieces in which they introduce the topic or book they are writing about, state an opinion, supply reasons that support the opinion, use linking words (e.g., because, and, also) to connect opinion and reasons, and provide a concluding statement or section.

Note that in kindergarten, students are expected to state an opinion about a specific book, whether through writing, drawing, or speaking. By first grade, they are expected to write, state an opinion about a specific book, supply a reason for their opinion, and close the piece in some way. By second grade, they are expected to supply multiple reasons, use linking words to connect reasons and opinions, and compose a purposeful conclusion. These nuances represent the cognitive progression across the grade levels. Teachers must consider whether or not students have mastered the prerequisite skills (the prior year's standard) and attend to providing learning and practice activities to achieve the current-year standard, with an eye on what will be expected of the student in the following year.

Table 4.3 offers a chart for identifying a standard (middle column) and then locating the standard from the prior grade (left column) and the next grade (right column). This chart offers a perspective in terms of where the grade-level standard fits into the bigger picture.

Table 4.3 Cognitive Progression in the CCSS: A Three-Year View

CCSS Progression Analysis: A Three-Year View
Understanding Nuances and Complexities

Progression Types:
  Extended Content—Additional skills and concepts introduced
  Higher Cognitive Levels—Greater levels of higher-order thinking required
  Metacognition—Thinking about the thinking/learning process required

Grade Level Before Yours:	Your Grade Level:	Grade Level Beyond Yours:
Standard: W.2.2—Write informative/explanatory texts in which they introduce a topic, *use facts and definitions to develop points*, and provide a concluding statement or section.	**Standard:** W.3.2b—*Develop the topic* with facts, definitions, and details. **Progression Type(s):** Higher Cognitive—"develop" indicates a flow in the writing in which facts, definitions, and details continue to be introduced to build on the topic **Evidence:** description of community resource that includes facts, definitions, and details	**Standard:** W.4.2b—Develop the topic with facts, definitions, *concrete details, quotations, or other information and examples* related to the topic. **Progression Type(s):** Extended content, i.e. quotes, examples, concrete details **Evidence:** description of community resource that includes all of the above

As you consider the move from one level to another, identify the type of progression from grade to grade. "Extended Content" indicates new content that builds on the standard; "Higher Cognitive Levels" indicates a deepening of understanding and an increase in complexity of thinking related to the standard; "Metacognition" indicates a focus on reflection on the power and use of the standard. The progression type provides insight into the types of instructional activities needed. Moving to extended content requires activities that allow the student to explore new content; moving to a higher cognitive level requires activities that promote higher-order thinking about learned content; and moving to a metacognitive level requires activities that promote thinking about learning processes and reflection on learning. For example, if students understand the concept of the volume of a rectangular prism (such as that of a cereal box or concrete step), the next curricular goal might be to calculate the volume of a cylinder. This activity requires extended content, so instructional activities might include having students grapple with figuring out the volume of a cylinder using paper models, watching a video explaining the calculation, and writing out the process for the calculation. Alternatively, the next curricular goal might be one of higher cognitive levels asking students to determine volume when another rectangular prism is cut out of the first. For example, imagine a cereal box with a 2" × 4" cutout near the top for use in creating a handle for carrying. To calculate the volume of the cereal box, students would have to calculate the volume of the box as if there were no cutout and then subtract the volume of the cutout. Instructional activities would need to include those that ask students to analyze the situation, given what they know about volume; work with models; hypothesize and test those hypotheses; and so forth. This would not be the time to offer students an explanation, as it would if offering extended content. This is the time to pose questions that prompt higher-order thinking. Finally, the next curricular goal might be to consider how to best describe the process of calculating the volume of a rectangular prism to others. Metacognition requires activities that engage students in reflection and deconstructing their own thinking processes: thinking about thinking.

Regardless of the subject area, you can identify the progression from one curricular objective to another and one grade level to another. This will help instructional activities to maximize student achievement.

Table 4.4 offers a chart for following an ELA standard from kindergarten through twelfth grade. Again, at each grade level, you can identify the progression to gain a better understanding of the learning activities needed to accomplish that level of understanding.

Table 4.4 CCSS Progression Analysis K-12 ELA

One of the shifts of the CCSS is that there is a clear progression of mastery and learning. The three types of progression can be categorized as follows:

Extended Content—Additional skills and concepts introduced

Higher Cognitive Level—Greater level of higher-order thinking required

Metacognition—Thinking about the thinking/learning process

The standards below are taken from the ELA Strand, **Reading Informational Text**, standard #6 (CCSS.ELA-Literacy.RI.K.6). Read each standard and record the type of progression in the chart below.

Standard		Progression
K:	Name the author and illustrator of a text and define the role of each in presenting the ideas or information in a text.	
1:	Distinguish between information provided by pictures or other illustrations and information provided by the words in a text.	Higher Cognitive Levels
2:	Identify the main purpose of a text, including what the author wants to answer, explain, or describe.	Extended Content
3:	Distinguish their own point of view from that of the author of a text.	Metacognition
4:	Compare and contrast a firsthand and secondhand account of the same event or topic; describe the differences in focus and the information provided.	Extended Content
5:	Analyze multiple accounts of the same event or topic, noting important similarities and differences in the point of view they represent.	Higher Cognitive Level
6:	Determine an author's point of view or purpose in a text and explain how it is conveyed in the text.	Higher Cognitive Level
7:	Determine an author's point of view or purpose in a text and analyze how the author distinguishes his or her position from that of others.	Higher Cognitive Level
8:	Determine an author's point of view or purpose in a text and analyze how the author acknowledges and responds to conflicting evidence or viewpoints.	Higher Cognitive Level
9–10:	Determine an author's point of view or purpose in a text and analyze how the author uses rhetoric to advance that point of view or purpose.	Extended Content
11–12:	Determine an author's point of view or purpose in a text in which the rhetoric is particularly effective, analyzing how style and content contribute to the power, persuasiveness, or beauty of the text.	Higher Cognitive Level

Cognitive Progression Across the Grade Levels in the Math Standards

Unlike the ELA standards, the CCSS math standards drop and add domains across the grade levels; thus, the math standards require a longer and more nuanced view. It is important to look at the high school standards, which are grouped by topical courses, to determine the progression from expected understandings developed in prior years. For example, a high school geometry standard on congruence reads:

> Use geometric descriptions of rigid motions to transform figures and to predict the effect of a given rigid motion on a given figure; given two figures, use the definition of congruence in terms of rigid motions to decide if they are congruent.

Working backwards, three standards in grade eight directly prepare students to move to the more complex understanding expected in high school:

♦ Understand that a two-dimensional figure is congruent to another if the second can be obtained from the first by a sequence of rotations, reflections, and translations; given two congruent figures, describe a sequence that exhibits the congruence between them.

♦ Describe the effect of dilations, translations, rotations, and reflections on two-dimensional figures using coordinates.

♦ Understand that a two-dimensional figure is similar to another if the second can be obtained from the first by a sequence of rotations, reflections, translations, and dilations; given two similar two-dimensional figures, describe a sequence that exhibits the similarity between them.

The concept of symmetry, a foundational match concept for higher-level geometry, is introduced in fourth grade, with the "matching parts" relating to congruence:

> Recognize a line of symmetry for a two-dimensional figure as a line across the figure such that the figure can be folded along the line into matching parts. Identify line-symmetric figures and draw lines of symmetry.

In kindergarten, students engage with geometric figures in ways that provide a foreshadowing of skills to come. As students analyze individual geometric figures, they'll begin to notice symmetry; as they analyze multiple figures, they'll begin to notice congruence, though neither of these terms will be introduced in kindergarten:

> Analyze and compare two- and three-dimensional shapes, in different sizes and orientations, using informal language to describe their similarities, differences, parts (e.g., number of sides and vertices/"corners") and other attributes (e.g., having sides of equal length).

The math standards in the early grades are critical for building the level of understanding needed in the upper grades. Consider this first-grade measurement and data standard:

> Order three objects by length; compare the lengths of two objects indirectly by using a third object.

Given three rods of varying lengths, students would first order them from shortest to longest. The second half of the standard is an introduction to the principle of transitivity, an early step in building logic. Though students don't need to know the term at this point, they will apply this concept when developing geometric proofs in high school. The CCSS seek to introduce advanced concepts in the early grades and build upon them through the years. In this case, if the yellow rod is shorter than the purple rod, and the purple rod is shorter than the black rod, one can logically deduce that the yellow rod is shorter than the black rod. That is the principle of transitivity, which, in this case, can be written as if $A < B$ and $B < C$ then $A < C$. The standard sounds more daunting than it actually is. This is the type of deduction that a first grader can make. To address this standard, students must engage with multiple sets of objects, ordering the objects and making observations and deductions.

Mapping the cognitive progression across the years is a little more difficult than with the ELA standards, as they can cross domains. Table 4.5

Table 4.5 CCSS Progression Analysis K-12 Math

Unlike the ELA standards, the math standards drop and add domains across the grade levels. Early foundations in the math standards pave the way for more complex understandings in later years. Using a math standard, determine at which prior grade levels it is "foreshadowed," "introduced," or "expanded."

Standard	Introduced/Foreshadowed/ Expanded
K: OA.A.2—Solve addition and subtraction word problems, and add and subtract within 10, e.g., by using objects or drawings to represent the problem.	Foreshadowed
1: OA.A.1—Use addition and subtraction within 20 to solve word problems involving situations of adding to, taking from, putting together, taking apart, and comparing, with unknowns in all positions, e.g., by using objects, drawings, and equations with a symbol for the unknown number to represent the problem.	Foreshadowed
2: OA.A.1—Use addition and subtraction within 100 to solve one- and two-step word problems involving situations of adding to, taking from, putting together, taking apart, and comparing, with unknowns in all positions, e.g., by using drawings and equations with a symbol for the unknown number to represent the problem.	Foreshadowed
3: OA.A.3—Use multiplication and division within 100 to solve word problems in situations involving equal groups, arrays, and measurement quantities, e.g., by using drawings and equations with a symbol for the unknown number to represent the problem.	Foreshadowed
4: OA.A.3—Solve multistep word problems posed with whole numbers and having whole-number answers using the four operations, including problems in which remainders must be interpreted. Represent these problems using equations with a letter standing for the unknown quantity. Assess the reasonableness of answers using mental computation and estimation strategies including rounding.	Foreshadowed
5: OA.A.2—Write simple expressions that record calculations with numbers, and interpret numerical expressions without evaluating them.	Foreshadowed

(*Continued*)

Table 4.5 *(Continued)*

Standard	Introduced/Foreshadowed/Expanded
6: EE.A.2.A—Write expressions that record operations with numbers and with letters standing for numbers. *For example, express the calculation "Subtract y from 5" as $5 - y$.*	Introduced
7: EE.A.1—Apply properties of operations as strategies to add, subtract, factor, and expand linear expressions with rational coefficients.	Expanded
8: EE.C.7.A—Give examples of linear equations in one variable with one solution, infinitely many solutions, or no solutions. Show which of these possibilities is the case by successively transforming the given equation into simpler forms, until an equivalent equation of the form $x = a$, $a = a$, or $a = b$ results (where a and b are different numbers).	Expanded
HS Number & Quantity:	
HS Algebra: REI.B.3—Solve linear equations and inequalities in one variable, including equations with coefficients represented by letters.	
HS Functions: N/A	
HS Modeling: N/A	
HS Geometry: N/A	
HS Statistics & Probability: ID.C.7—Interpret the slope (rate of change) and the intercept (constant term) of a linear model in the context of the data.	Expanded

offers a breakdown of a high school algebra standard related to solving linear equations (in bold print).

If you review the prior grades, writing equations with letters to represent unknown amounts is introduced in sixth grade and then expanded in grades seven and eight, progressing to linear equations in the eighth grade. Looking further back across the years, the ability to solve a word problem, including using symbols for unknown quantities, is a foreshadowing of skills to come.

Toward a Culture of Learning

As was stated at the beginning of this chapter, human beings love to learn. Classrooms should be places where students actively engage in learning, spurred on by their innate inquisitiveness and thirst for knowledge, not by compliance to adults. Teachers can create a culture of learning by taking into account the brain's natural tendency toward cognitive progression: Each new learning spawns a new quest for further learning. If curricular topics are introduced to leverage cognitive progression, the likelihood that students will achieve at high levels increases.

Your Turn
Cognitive Progression for Math

Identify a math standard that is of interest to you. Use the approach in Table 4.5 to map out the progression of this standard across the years, identifying where the actual skill or concept is introduced, where it is expanded upon, and where it is foreshadowed by other skills.

In Summary

Leveraging cognitive progression means:

♦ Considering how the mastery of a skill or concept begins with a simple understanding and levels up to more complex understandings

♦ Ensuring that students have opportunities to build incrementally upon their cognitive level of understanding of any concept or skill

♦ Attending to the cognitive load of information being presented to students, seeking to minimize it

♦ Identifying how a standard progresses across the grade levels

Chapter 5

The Fourth Insight

The Power of Language Transcends the Disciplines

Uttering a word is like striking a note on the keyboard of the imagination.

—Ludwig Wittgenstein

Babies first hear sounds when they are in the womb, at approximately four months. They may not understand exact word meanings, but they can process calmness, anger, joy, and other emotions from hearing their mother's voice. From birth, babies begin making connections between words and people, places, items, actions, relationships, and emotions. Although babies cannot speak, you should never underestimate how much they understand.

The human voice box sits lower in the throat than in that of any other primate, allowing humans to generate the wide range of sounds required for speech. However, at birth, a baby's voice box sits high in the throat, allowing the baby to breathe and swallow at the same time—an important capability for the nursing infant. A baby's voice box does not lower into the necessary position for complex speech until about nine months of age. In these early months, a baby learns to comprehend language and develops ideas, sentiments, and needs, but is unable to speak them.

Speech development begins the journey toward efficacy: the satisfying ability to produce a desired result. The further ability to read and write advances one in this goal. Language is a powerful tool that can be harnessed to produce great results; it allows one to make a difference in one's own life and the lives of others.

Everyday life is brimming with words: road signs, television ads, directions, questions, product labels, editorials, songs, friendly encounters, not-so-friendly encounters, world news, local news, family news, loving words, encouraging words, critical words, the words inside your head, and on and on. The brain processes an abundance of words every waking hour. It does not have to pause to overtly decide to read for information or for aesthetic enjoyment; it encounters myriad words of different message types in the course of the day and processes them accordingly. Language is a natural part of our lives and, as such, can be harnessed as a foundation to drive higher achievement.

The CCSS were written for two languages: English, the language through which we learn and communicate every day, and mathematics, the language through which we describe the natural world. Harnessing language toward student achievement includes:

- Purposeful reading of literature to develop character and experience upon which to build in the pursuit of advanced learning goals;

- Purposeful reading of informational text to advance learning across the content areas;

- The use of deliberate and precise language;

- Addressing the audience connection; and

- Viewing mathematics, and all subject areas, as languages.

The Power of Literature

Literature, in all its forms, is the venue through which we share the human experience. Brain research supports the need to engage with fiction as a means to develop socially and emotionally. "Lifetime exposure to narrative fiction . . . is positively associated with social abilities" (Mar, 2011, p. 110). Through the stories of others, fiction readers experience life, confront their own beliefs, feel the emotions of the characters, and respond to the characters as they would in real life; fiction essentially allows the reader to simulate real life and gain valuable social and emotional experiences. Through engaging with every type of literary text, the reader learns about the human experience. Fiction "measurably enhances our abilities to empathize with other people and connect with something larger than ourselves" (Oatley, 2009).

Consider the rise in popularity of dystopian literature in the pre-teen and adolescent populations (Miller, 2010). Novels such as *The Giver* and *The Hunger Games* are set in a time in the course of history when a utopian period of peace and prosperity has ended and the characters live in a world where injustice and oppression rule—a dysfunctional utopia, or dystopia. Yet, there is still a glimmer of hope for the main characters to overcome their circumstances. The adolescent years are typically a stage in which a young person feels that the carefree days of childhood are gone, replaced with a reality and rules that seem oppressive. Thus, many adolescents relate to literature that is dystopian. Fiction provides adolescents with the opportunity to work through life's changing times by living vicariously through fictional characters. Literature serves as a powerful venue for social and emotional growth, for imagining beyond the current reality. Reading a word can be "like striking a note on the keyboard of the imagination" (Wittgenstein, 1958, p. 4).

Fiction also stimulates the brain in ways that informational text cannot. Sensory words and metaphors, readily available in fiction, positively stimulate the brain, allowing the reader to make connections and deepen understanding. The brain treats sensory words as if it were actually experiencing the sensation. A summary of a study by researchers in Spain on the brain and fiction offers the following results:

> When subjects looked at the Spanish words for "perfume" and "coffee," their primary olfactory cortex lit up; when they saw the words that mean "chair" and "key," this region remained dark. The way the brain handles metaphors has also received extensive study. . . . Last month, however, a team of researchers from Emory University reported in Brain & Language that when subjects in their laboratory read a metaphor involving texture, the sensory cortex, responsible for perceiving texture through touch, became active. Metaphors like "The singer had a velvet voice" and "He had leathery hands" roused the sensory cortex, while phrases matched for meaning, like "The singer had a pleasing voice" and "He had strong hands," did not.
>
> (Paul, 2012, p. 6)

Consider the implications for learning. Fiction has the power to change the reader, providing a wealth of experiences otherwise unattainable in one's life. To do so, the reader must uncover the meaning presented in the text through purposeful reading. Purposeful reading of literature involves imagining—that is, creating a mental picture of the events of the story and becoming emotionally engaged. These mental pictures emerge from the words on the page. While consuming the text, the reader may feel amused, saddened, angry, nervous, and so forth. Purposeful reading of literature includes making connections: text to text, text to self, text to world. The very nature of literature is to capture and share experiences; purposeful reading includes making important connections to further understanding. Teachers can help students harness the power of literature in their lives by providing them with structures for making those connections. The standards do not end with these connections; if anything, they begin with them. Such connections allow students to relate to the material, thus allowing the material to make sense and take on personal meaning. Next, the student can delve more deeply into the higher-level thinking of the CCSS themselves. (Note: this book is not intended to provide a comprehensive analysis of all of the standards, but rather insights that will help unleash the power of the CCSS.)

A concise reflection chart (see Table 5.1), modified to suit the grade level, will focus students on the power of words to allow them to make those connections. Students make connections and identify the words and phrases that led to those connections. Teachers should make their thinking transparent as they share the connections they make to the text and the words that led to those connections. Students can consider how characters in the story relate to the events in the same way or differently from the way they relate. As students shift to writing, they can think about what emotions they wish to elicit and the imagery they want to create, then consider the words that would accomplish the goal.

This approach helps students at all grade levels make the connections they need to build their comprehension when reading literature. The second column is meant to focus them in on how the author creates meaning for the reader; however, the column could be modified to address other questions, such as, "how does the main character react to the situation compared to how you react to it?" or "what can you predict will happen later?"

The meaning of an excerpt of literature is often more elusive than that of informational text. Authors of literature convey meaning through a variety of literary devices, including the use of figurative language to create greater imagery. Authors of informational text primarily use literal

Table 5.1 Literature: Text Connections

	Connection: *This reminds me of . . .*	**Powerful Words and Imagery**
Text to Text		
Text to Self		
Text to World		

language that should be taken at face value, with some use of figurative language—such as metaphor, for example—to make a point. Students need to harness the power of figurative language: alliteration, hyperbole, imagery, idiom, irony, metaphor, onomatopoeia, oxymoron, personification, pun, and simile, for example. They must understand how to read words in context so they can determine whether they are reading figurative or literal language. For example, the statement, "You hit the nail on the head" could mean, figuratively, you accurately identified the issue, or it could mean literally, you successfully struck a nail with the hammer. The only way to determine the meaning is to consider the context within which the statement is used. Purposeful reading includes using context to determine the meaning of figurative language to further understanding. Teachers can help students harness the power of literature in their lives by providing them with structures for determining the meaning of words and phrases.

A "tone and meaning chart" (see Table 5.2), which should be modified to suit each grade level, will focus students on the power of words to create tone and meaning. This particular chart would be appropriate for students in fifth grade and beyond.

Consider the end-goal of CCSS.ELA-LIT.RL.6.4, discussed in chapter 2:

Determine the meaning of words and phrases as they are used in a text, including figurative and connotative meanings; analyze the impact of a specific word choice on meaning and tone.

The emphasis is on creating tone and meaning through specific word choice—the end-goal of the standard. Students should identify which type of figurative language is used, driving the need to learn the various types. English Language Learners could create a physical or digital word wall of idioms, metaphors, and similes with illustrations. As students shift to writing, they should be guided to think about what tone and meaning they wish to convey, and then consider the figurative language that would accomplish the goal.

ELA Reading Literature standard 1 addresses citing evidence from text based on explicit meaning. As students learn to uncover the meaning of words, they should be guided to focus on how the author uses words to convey actions and situations in the past, present, and future through both explicit statements and inference. The graphic organizer

Table 5.2 Literature: Figurative Language

Excerpt (page and paragraph)	Word choice and conveyed tone or meaning	Alliteration	Hyperbole	Imagery	Idiom	Irony	Metaphor	Onomatopoeia	Oxymoron	Personification	Pun	Simile

in Table 5.3 can be used to connect explicit text and inferences to past, present, and predicted events.

Table 5.3 Literature: Explicit Language vs. Inference

	Explicit	**Inference**
I know what happened in the past because of the words:		
I know what is happening in the present because of the words:		
I can imagine or know what might happen in the future because of the words:		

Your Turn
Harnessing the Power of Language Through Literature

Consider how the three graphic organizers in Tables 5.1, 5.2, and 5.3 help students address the standards while experiencing the power of literature. Identify a piece of literature of interest to you. It does not have to be related to English class; it could be historical fiction, science fiction, a story in which the main character is an artist, etc. Design an original graphic organizer for one of the nine standards for reading literature. First, be sure to distinguish between the end-goal of the standard and the means. Then, determine how you could categorize or graphically depict the standard so that students build understanding.

Purposeful Reading of Informational Text

The CCSS offer 10 standards that are similar to those for reading literature, with slight modifications for informational text, plus the additional standard of tracing and evaluating arguments and claims made based on reasoning and sufficiency of supportive evidence. Teachers can use similar graphic organizers as those presented in Tables 5.1, 5.2, and 5.3 when teaching students to harness the power of words in informational text.

People typically read informational text for a purpose: to learn about a topic, to uncover specific information to use to build a case, or to master a skill. Informational text employs five structures to convey the content:

♦ Description

♦ Sequence

- Compare and contrast

- Cause and effect

- Problem and solution

These structures are characterized by cue words that alert the reader to the structure being used, aiding in overall comprehension and retention of the text. For example, the sequence structure includes cue words such as first, second, finally, next, following, subsequently, before, and so forth. The reader encounters these words and knows that the text is addressing the sequence of events or information. A recipe relies heavily on the sequence structure, as does a technical how-to document, a biography, and so forth.

All of these structures can appear in the same text, so students must learn strategies for uncovering information via these various structures. One document will most likely contain multiple structures, and the reader must recognize when the structure has changed. The "informational text structures" chart (Table 5.4) offers an overview of each type of structure.

Table 5.4 Informational Text: Structures

Type of Structure	Cue Word Examples	Where Typically Found
Description— main ideas followed by details, descriptive adjectives, and words that use the five senses to convey meaning	for instance, such as, specifically, also	travel guides, advertisements, art critiques, books about animals, trade books, etc.
Sequence— a set of steps or information written chronologically	first, second, next, finally, before, after, following	recipes, how-to books, historical accounts, biographies, directions, technical manuals, etc.
Compare and Contrast— similarities and differences between or among choices, items, people, and ideas	similar to, different from, as opposed to, on the other hand, both, in contrast, too	product reviews, opinion pieces, historical accounts, critiques, etc.
Cause and Effect— outcomes of an event or action, a single event or action being the cause, and the outcome(s) being the effect	because, leads to, produces, consequently, as a result of, if . . . then, results in, creates, causes	current events, historical accounts, scientific explanation, etc.
Problem and Solution— describes a problem and offers one or more possible solutions	purpose, conclude, perhaps, idea, consequently, solve, solution, then	opinion pieces, product advertisements, self-help books, etc.

Students can build this chart, adding more cue words and examples as they encounter more texts. They can apply this knowledge and the skill of identifying informational text structures as they read. For example, the text displayed in Table 5.5 is an excerpt from www.howstuffworks.com. The italicized words are the cues introducing different text structures. Note how often the structure will change in a single excerpt of text and the type of information that is provided with each different structure.

Students can use the same format as in Table 5.5 to map out the structures in an excerpt from an informational text they are reading. Teachers may want to add a third column in which students take notes on what they learned, highlighting the importance of having an internal conversation with the text, and fostering text annotation.

Informational text standard 3 requires students to analyze the interactions among characters, events, ideas, or pieces of information. Figures 5.1, 5.2, and 5.3 offer graphic organizers at the first-, fifth-, and ninth/tenth-grade

Table 5.5   Informational Text: Sample Text

In the broad expanse of the northern Pacific Ocean, *there exists* the North Pacific Subtropical Gyre, a slowly moving, clockwise spiral of currents	Descriptive
created by a high-pressure system of air currents. *The area is* an **oceanic desert**, filled with tiny phytoplankton	Cause and Effect Descriptive
but few big fish or mammals. *Due to* its lack of large fish and gentle breezes, fishermen and sailors rarely	Cause and Effect
travel through the gyre. But *the area* is filled with something besides plankton: trash, millions of pounds of	Descriptive
it, most of all plastic. It's *the largest* landfill in the world, and it floats in the middle of the ocean . . .	Compare and Contrast
Nearly all experts who speak about the subject raise the same point: *It comes down to* managing waste on land, where most of the	Problem and Solution
trash originates. They *recommend* lobbying companies to find alternatives to plastic, especially environmentally safe, reusable packaging. Recycling programs should be expanded to accommodate more types of plastic, and the public must be educated about their value.	Problem and Solution

Figure 5.1   Informational Text: Primary Graphic Organizer

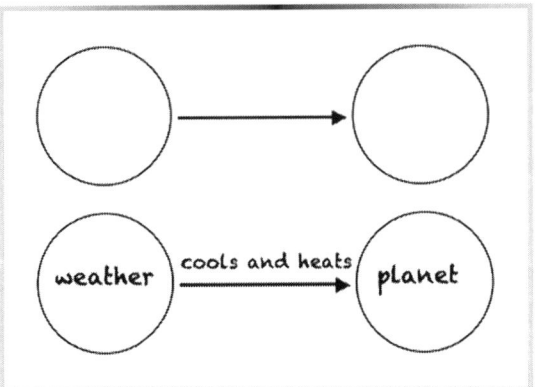

levels to demonstrate that a graphic organizer can be modified to address the nuances introduced in a standard across the years.

The graphic organizer in Figure 5.1 asks first-graders to select two characters, events, ideas, or pieces of information and shows the relationship of one to the other. The completed diagram is an example from a non-fiction book on storms. The student reads the sentence, "Weather cools and heats our planet so it is just right for life" (Goin, 2009, p. 5) and selects the two ideas, or concepts: weather and planet. The student has to describe, from the text, the connection between the weather and the planet.

By the fifth grade, this same standard now requires students to:

> Explain the relationships or interactions between two or more individuals, events, ideas, or concepts in a historical, scientific, or technical text based on specific information in the text.

The graphic organizer would expand to include more than one item or require the student to consider the dual impact one item has on the other, and vice versa (see Figure 5.2). In this standard, students must recognize the words that convey relationships, including cause-and-effect relationships that are typical of historical, scientific, and technical texts.

By the ninth and tenth grades, the standard requires students to:

> Analyze how the author unfolds an analysis or series of ideas or events, including the order in which the points are made, how they are introduced and developed, and the connections that are drawn between them.

The graphic organizer would now be either a longer chain of ideas or events, or a smaller number requiring the student to identify the interde-

Figure 5.2   Informational Text: Intermediate Graphic Organizer

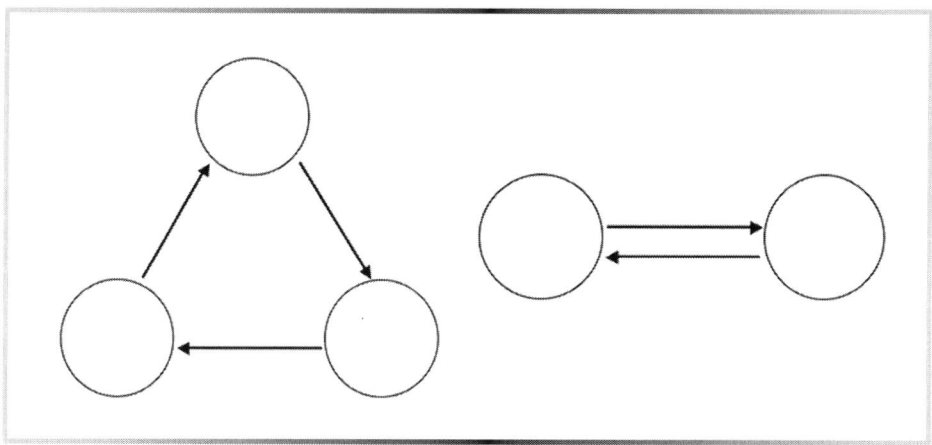

Figure 5.3   Informational Text: High School Graphic Organizer

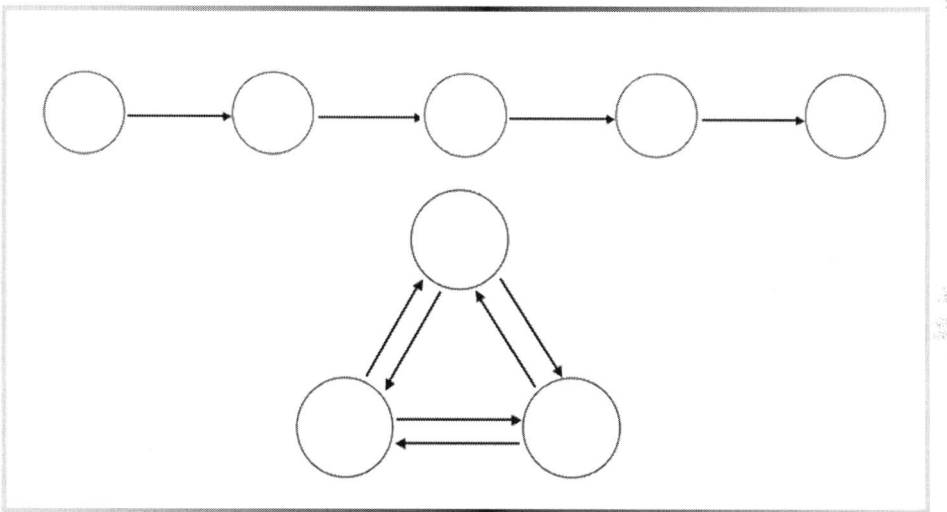

pendencies of each to all others shown (see Figure 5.3). The student would then analyze how the author depicts these relationships in the text.

Graphic organizers are a powerful way to focus students on grasping the meaning of words in addressing the various standards. Given that the ELA standards become more demanding and more sophisticated over the years, the graphic organizer, too, must accommodate this greater complexity.

Your Turn
Helping Students Read Informational Text Purposefully

Design a graphic organizer for a subject area and grade level that addresses one or more of the standards in terms of the power of informational text to convey meaning.

Viewing Mathematics, and Other Subject Areas, as a Language

The CCSS currently focus on mastering the art of communication in two languages: English and mathematics. This section will address mathematics, but you can consider how the points made apply to other subject areas.

Most people may not initially think of mathematics as a language, but it is, in fact, the language that describes the natural world and its relationships. Consider the following:

♦ A square window is divided into six rectangular panes

♦ 80% of the class prefer chocolate ice cream to vanilla

♦ Joaquin ate three quarters of the candy bar

♦ The room is 80 feet by 37 feet

♦ The area of the round carpet is πr^2, that is, pi times a radius of 4 feet squared

♦ The height of the tower is 80 times the tangent of 40 degrees

All of these statements are descriptions using mathematical terms. They express quantities, relationships, and measurements. Mathematics is a descriptive language.

Two dimes plus a nickel equals 25 cents. If you double the dimes and nickels to four dimes plus two nickels, you end up with twice 25 cents, or 50 cents. A relationship exists. Let's represent dimes by the variable x and nickels by the variable y. We started with two dimes plus a nickel equals 25 cents, or $2x + y = 25$. We then doubled the amounts to $4x + 2y = 50$. If we increase the number of dimes and nickels from the original number fourfold, we would have $8x + 4y = 100$. Sure enough, if you have eight dimes (80 cents) and four nickels (20 cents), you have a dollar (100 cents), or four times 25 cents. A relationship exists that can either be described in English using a number of words, or mathematically using a few symbols.

The language of mathematics provides an efficient communication tool for representing, analyzing, and solving problems using relationships among quantities in the world.

A second-grade teacher asks students to describe themselves using numbers: their height, their weight, the length of their arms, the distance between their eyes, the number of siblings they have, the number of steps they take to walk to school, and so forth. The students are encouraged to be as creative as they can, as long as they are using numbers for their descriptions, and the information is appropriate to be shared in school. Next, the teacher asks the students to write sentences about the relationship between their numbers and those of their classmates. Students write relationship descriptions, such as, "3 of us are 40 inches tall," "I am four inches shorter than Jamal," "6 of us have 2 siblings," "I have twice as many siblings as Jason," and, with further prompting, descriptions such as, "I have twice as many siblings as 4 of my classmates." The lesson extends to exploring comparisons, such as, "3 of the 24 of us are 38 inches tall," and "6 of 24 of us have 2 siblings." Manipulatives allow students to explore these relationships further. As you can imagine, the possibilities are endless for exploring descriptions and comparisons, representing the information in graphs, and writing and solving equations using mathematical notation. Math is a language of conservation; that is, one can typically express relationships using fewer symbols than words.

Mathematical notation is universal, allowing those who speak different languages to still communicate using the global language of mathematics. Given that language is all around us, looking at mathematics and other subject areas as descriptive languages may make it easier for some students to embrace what otherwise feels like unattainable concepts and skills made up of numbers, symbols, formulas, and theorems.

Solving Real-World Problems

Consider the following eighth-grade standard:

> Understand that a function is a rule that assigns to each input exactly one output. The graph of a function is the set of ordered pairs consisting of an input and the corresponding output.

A car's gas mileage can be written as a function. If a car gets 21 miles to the gallon, the total number of miles to be driven on the remaining gas in the tank can be written as the function $y = 21x$, where y is the total miles and x is the number of gallons of gas left in the tank. In identifying the ordered pairs, students can use a chart (see Table 5.6).

Table 5.6 Chart: Gallons of Gas/Miles to Drive

x (gallons of gas)	y (miles to drive)
1	21
2	42
3	63
4	84

Students should be able to discuss the relationship between the number of gallons of gas left and the total miles that can be driven as a result. Students should also be able to explain why, for each value of x, there is a unique value of y. Real-world scenarios foster the use of math as a descriptive language.

Consider the following high-school standard:

Use matrices to represent and manipulate data.

A hotdog vendor tracks his food sales per week for three weeks (Table 5.7). He also tracks his cost to produce each food item (Table 5.8).

Table 5.7 Chart: Hotdog Vendor's Sales

	Week 1	Week 2	Week 3
Hotdogs	220	232	215
Fries	180	200	210
Soda	240	225	235

Table 5.8 Chart: Hotdog Vendor's Costs

	Week 1	Week 2	Week 3
Hotdogs	.40	.42	.42
Fries	.10	.10	.12
Soda	.18	.20	.21

Figure 5.4 Matrices

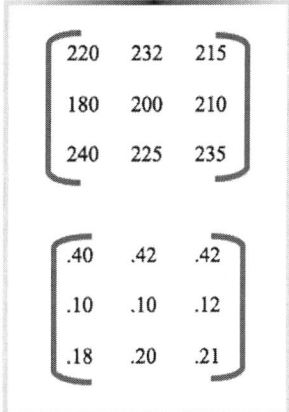

The student can set up a matrix for each (or a pair of matrices) to mathematically represent this data (see Figure 5.4).

From here, further conversations around the data can lead to the development of equations and multiplication of matrices using this data. Using mathematics will allow students, on behalf of the vendor, to analyze sales and make decisions. Teachers and students pose questions to probe thinking, leading to a deeper understanding.

Focusing on mathematics as a language also forces students to talk about and write about the world around them using domain specific language. Moving away from rote calculations, students will discuss situations using the language of mathematics, which will drive them to a deeper understanding of concepts.

Your Turn
Practicing the Language of Mathematics

Look around you. Try to describe what you see in mathematical terms, first with language and then with expressions and mathematical notation.

Using Deliberate and Precise Language

One way in which writers and speakers harness the power of language is through deliberate and precise word choice. Effective writing requires far more than the creativity, five paragraphs, and mechanics that have dominated most writing programs. It requires the writer to consider the "why"

Table 5.9 Three Types of Writing

Type of Writing	The "Why"	The "How"
Argument Writing	Convince others to agree with you.	Present compelling facts in a way that allows the audience to reason its way to agreeing with you, erasing all doubt you may not be right.
Informative/Explanatory	Educate others on a topic.	Present critical information in a way that builds others' knowledge base.
Narrative	Tell a story.	Retell the events of the story in a way that lets others visualize and comprehend it.

of the piece, apply the "how" to develop a strategy for addressing the intended audience and purpose, and choose deliberate and precise words.

The CCSS captures the "why" of writing by assigning all writing to one of three categories: argument writing, informative/explanatory writing, and narrative writing, depicted in Table 5.9. Each of the three writing categories requires the use of deliberate and precise language.

The kindergarten standard for argument writing expects the student to state an opinion. By fifth grade, the student must back up the opinion with "logically ordered reasons that are supported by facts and details." At the sixth-grade level, the word "opinion" is replaced with "argument"; the eleventh/twelfth-grade standard expects the student to write well-constructed arguments that support claims and develop counterclaims, anticipating the audience's reaction.

The kindergarten standard for informative/explanatory writing expects the student to name a subject and share something about it. By fifth grade, the student must develop the topic with "facts, definitions, concrete details, quotations, or other information and examples." The student must "use precise language and domain-specific vocabulary." The eleventh/twelfth-grade standard expects the student additionally to "organize complex ideas, concepts, and information so that each new element builds on that which precedes it to create a unified whole" and "use precise language, domain-specific vocabulary, and techniques such as metaphor, simile, and analogy to manage the complexity of the topic."

The kindergarten standard for narrative writing expects the student to share a series of events in order and provide a reaction to what happened. By fifth grade, the student must "develop real or imagined experiences or events using effective technique, descriptive details, and clear event sequences." The student must "use concrete words and phrases and sensory details to convey experiences and events precisely." The eleventh/twelfth-grade standard expects the student additionally to "use a variety of techniques to sequence events so that they build on one another to create a coherent whole and build toward a particular tone and outcome" and "use precise words and phrases, telling details, and sensory language to convey a vivid picture of the experiences, events, setting, and/or characters."

Words Matter

The CCSS distinguish among everyday, academic, and domain-specific vocabulary. Academic and domain-specific vocabulary allow students to be deliberate and precise in their communication. The use of academic and domain-specific vocabulary begins with the teacher's modeling. Teachers may tend to use vocabulary that they know their students will readily understand; after all, it seems counterproductive to continually use words that are unknown to students, as they would be frustrated and it would impede learning. It is, however, incumbent upon teachers to raise the level of vocabulary use in the classroom to harness the power of language for their students. Here are five strategies for building a culture of deliberate and precise word choice in the classroom:

1. **Develop a three-tier vocabulary chart:** Teachers can think through a unit of study and develop a three-tier chart (see Table 5.10). They should consider the everyday language they might expect students to use during the unit, then brainstorm academic and domain-specific vocabulary to be introduced. They may want to use a thesaurus to explore words from the everyday vocabulary list to determine which new academic vocabulary they can introduce. This will offer a guide for modeling word choices in written and oral communication with students. It will also provide them with words for the classroom "word wall."

2. **Introduce new words by using them and immediately defining them.** For example, as teachers introduce a challenge to students, they might say, "Above all, be tenacious! . . . Stick with it, don't give up, be persistent." They should avoid offering up the first sentence and then saying, "Who knows what 'tenacious' means?" Students who fail to recognize the word may feel defeated and embarrassed. Instead, teachers can combine the new word with its meaning in order to build vocabulary. As soon as teachers utter the new word, their students' brains will experience cognitive dissonance—a gap between what they know and don't know,

Table 5.10 Three Tiers of Vocabulary

Directions: The CCSS focus on literacy across the content areas. Vocabulary acquisition is a critical factor in improving literacy. Focused vocabulary instruction increases academic rigor and leads to better comprehension of text in any subject area. Read the Three Tiers of Vocabulary definitions below. Then identify words for each tier related to an upcoming unit of study.

Tier	Tier 1—Basic Vocabulary	Tier 2—Academic Vocabulary	Tier 3—Domain-Specific Vocabulary
Definition	Basic words that one encounters frequently; requires little instruction. Examples: table, dance, book, dog, old	High-frequency words found across a variety of knowledge domains. Examples: abstract, requirement, method, symbol	Low-frequency words used for a specific area or knowledge domain. Examples: isosceles, erosion, stanza, archipelago
Unit of Study: _____			

a requirement for learning to take place. It is important to pause for a full second (to say "one hundred one" to oneself to fill that second) before offering the follow-up explanation. That way, students' brains can experience the cognitive dissonance and be in "search mode" for the answer. When they then hear the definition, they will experience a silent "ahhhh." Another one-second pause will allow students to think through the word they just learned. In the above example case, the teacher might continue with, "Your tenacity will pay off," offering students a look at various grammatical forms of the word.

3. **Create a "graduated word wall," either physically or digitally**. This strategy encourages students to identify higher-level words to use that are more precise in meaning. In Table 5.11, the columns are labeled "good," "more precise," and "even more precise." In a primary-level classroom, teachers might exchange those headings for "good," "better," and "even better." Note that no "best" exists because students can always find an even better word. As demonstrated in the example, some words, such as "hard," have multiple meanings based on context. Using a more precise word will allow

Table 5.11 Precise Language Chart

Good	More Precise	Even More Precise
Hard	Tough	Challenging
Hard	Solid	Impervious
Good	Tasty	Scrumptious

the reader to easily understand meaning. In the first example, the word "hard" is used to describe a math problem. In the second, the word is used to describe a rock sample. In the third, the word "good" is used to describe the taste of a cookie. This approach will create a culture of word refinement with students being challenged to continuously seek out alternative words.

4. **Challenge students, and oneself, to replace the overused, vague words, such as "do" and "thing."** These words are imprecise; the audience would benefit from further refining. "Do a survey" becomes "Conduct a survey" or "Respond to a survey." "Do this activity in your group" becomes "Complete . . ." or "Engage in this activity with your group members." "The hardest thing to do is . . ." becomes "The most challenging activity is . . ." Joining with students in the challenge to eliminate overused words can be gratifying and fun (I mean, interesting . . . engaging.)

5. **Challenge your students, and yourself, to eliminate the qualifiers "very," "really," and "totally" from their vocabulary.** Mark Twain is quoted as saying, "Substitute 'damn' every time you're inclined to write 'very'; your editor will delete it and the writing will be just as it should be." You might institute a "Very" word wall in which students identify current uses and a replacement vocabulary word. For example, "very hungry" becomes "famished"; "very long" becomes "lengthy"; "very happy" become ecstatic. Search and replace!

Your Turn
Modeling Deliberate and Precise Language

Identify a lesson on a topic of interest and write out what you might say to students. Then revise it to model the use of deliberate and precise language. Use the "Three Tiers of Vocabulary" to consider what academic and domain-specific vocabulary you can build into your own usage to introduce the content to students.

Making the Audience Connection

No matter what the content, writing is not merely a matter of fingers to keyboard; nor is speaking a matter of simply opening one's mouth. Prior to engaging in either, the writer or speaker needs to take into account the purpose, topic, and audience in order to make decisions about structure and word choice. The audience, and thus the author's choices, differs among the various types of writing: scholarly writing, formal writing, literary writing, informal writing, digital writing, and digital chatter. A formal letter might include, "I await the next opportunity to discuss this matter in person." An informal letter might include, "Looking forward to seeing you soon to talk more." Digital chatter might include, "c u l8r." Audience plays a role in structure and word choice.

A writer must take into account the perspective of the audience. An article on the importance of exercise, for example, will be written differently depending on whether the audience is a group of first-grade students, senior citizens, overweight people, athletes, or disabled persons. This book would be written differently were the intended audience students. A speech on the need for clean water will vary depending on whether the audience is a group of students, a company that contributes to water pollution, citizens of a third-world country, or politicians. Problem-solvers, innovators, and entrepreneurs must communicate effectively to a variety of audiences for a variety of purposes. It is not enough to master the basic rules of grammar and paragraph construction. Structure, vocabulary, word choices, and message progression are tools of a writer or speaker—tools that, when used deliberately to address the demands of the audience, content, and purpose, allow the writer or speaker to harness the power of language.

A simple exercise along these lines is to ask students to write or prepare three speeches on the same topic for three different audiences. For example, if students are studying French culture in preparation for receiving exchange students, they can write speeches for the students in their own school, for school board members, and for the French students. The message to students in the school would educate them and offer suggestions for making the visitors feel welcome; the message to school board members might address the value of having exchange students or reasons to eliminate the program; the message to the French students might be to welcome them and offer advice for their first days. In each case, have students reflect on and share their deliberate word choices based on the audience, the content they chose to share based on the audience, and how they feel they met the needs of the particular audience.

Far too many classroom assignments go no further than the teacher's desk; the audience is always the same. Making the audience connection relies on providing students with opportunities to address task, purpose, and audience by offering them opportunities to write to those outside the classroom. Students might write to or videoconference with a company representative, relative, student in another school, newspaper editor, government official, younger students, older students, and so forth. In each case, students should be guided to ensure that they take into account how the writing will differ given their audience.

Your Turn
Addressing the Audience Connection

Design a writing assignment for students in any content area that allows them to target a specific type of audience. Develop a graphic organizer that will guide them in brainstorming the content that would be most meaningful to the audience and words that would be appropriate for the audience.

Your Turn
Harnessing the Power of Other Subject Areas as Languages

Select a subject area of interest to you other than ELA or mathematics. Brainstorm how it operates as a language.

In Summary

Harnessing the power of language means:

♦ Acknowledging the role of literature in the social and emotional growth of students toward academic achievement

♦ Helping students make connections to literature: text to text, text to self, text to world

♦ Helping students identify how the use of figurative language builds tone and meaning

♦ Helping students identify explicit text from inference

- Helping students use the structures of informational text to make meaning

- Helping students see the connections among characters, events, ideas, or pieces of information

- Helping students understand the why and how of the three types of writing

- Viewing mathematics as the language that describes the real world

- Helping students to describe any subject-area content through mathematical terms

- Modeling the use of, and challenging students to locate and use, academic and domain-specific vocabulary

- Modeling the use of, and challenging students to use, deliberate and specific language

- Helping students use deliberate and specific language to address an audience

Chapter 6

The Fifth Insight

Executive Function Is Foundational for All Learning

The potential for greatness lives within each of us.
—*Wilma Rudolph*

The unique powers of the prefrontal cortex gave early humans the capability to construct tools, exercise self-control, and begin to control aspects of the environment around them. . . . but most of all it gave them the power of symbolic thought, which has become the basis of all human achievement since then.

(Jeremy, 2010)

Part of being human is the ability to manage information mentally and self-regulate in order to engage in high levels of complex thinking. The cognitive processes that fall under this umbrella are known as "executive function," and they are developed and strengthened as a person connects past experiences to the present to determine the best action to take. Being strategic, solving problems, setting goals and monitoring progress, creating and implementing a plan of action, analyzing and correcting errors, and controlling spontaneous reactions are some of the characteristics of executive function.

While schooling tends to focus on the transference of academic concepts, skills, and content, it is executive function that drives one's ability to achieve academically. Being able to make sense of a story book, scientific experiment, graph, chord progression in a song, or series of plays by a football team all require holding onto multiple pieces of information, reasoning, and focus—skills that fall under executive function. Making the CCSS work for you involves attending to the development of greater executive function in students.

Executive Function and Student Achievement

The CCSS are pushing a new level of standardized testing that focuses on applying content in ways that demonstrate deep understanding and draws on the work of Benjamin Bloom. Students cannot cram for or memorize the answers for the content that will appear on CCSS-aligned tests. Rather, questions tend to involve multi-step processing, requiring the application of content to a new situation, writing a new ending for a story, and so forth. Such higher-order thinking harkens to Bloom's Taxonomy, which presents a set of skills that require increasingly higher-order thinking: recall, comprehension, application, analysis, evaluation, and synthesis. (Note that "application," in this case, is the application of procedural learning.) The first three levels can be achieved largely through procedural automaticity; the next three require a much greater level of higher-order thinking, including cognitive flexibility, which enables creativity; working memory, which enables cause-and-effect thinking; and reflection. They require executive function. Bloom designed his taxonomy to represent increasingly higher-order levels of thinking, which he knew were characteristic of the human brain; what was still uncharted at the time was how the brain exhibited those levels of thinking.

Benjamin Bloom was 74 years old when Patricia Goldman-Rakic published her 1987 seminal research on mapping the prefrontal cortex of the brain—the center of executive function and the key to higher-order thinking. Key to students achieving the level of higher-order thinking required by the CCSS and emerging tests is the ability of teachers to realize that the progression to higher-order skills requires attention to executive function.

Think about the skills and habits you would consider to be important to success in school. How many of these abilities fit into your list?

♦ Concentration

♦ Attending to a person or activity

♦ Switching focus from one event to another

♦ Remembering details

♦ Managing time

♦ Working toward a goal

♦ Maintaining social control

♦ Considering future consequences in light of current action

♦ Analyzing

- Planning

- Reasoning

- Problem solving

- Predicting outcomes

- Managing conflicting thoughts

- Understanding same and different

- Seeing various possible solutions to a problem situation

- Inhibiting responses when necessary based on context

You would probably agree that all of these skills and habits are important, perhaps in varying degrees, for success in school. These are the skills that comprise executive function. Table 6.1 offers a categorized look at executive function.

Table 6.1 Executive Function

Organization	Cognitive Flexibility	Shifting focus from one event to another, changing perspective, seeing multiple sides to a situation, being open to others' points of view, being creative, catching and correcting errors, thinking about multiple concepts simultaneously
	Working Memory	Storing and manipulating visual and verbal information, identifying same and different, remembering details, following multiple steps, holding on to information while considering other information, identifying cause-and-effect relationships, categorizing information
	Planning	Setting goals, managing time, working towards a goal, organizing actions and thoughts, considering future consequences in light of current action
	Reasoning	Making hypotheses, deductions, and inferences; applying former approaches to new situations
	Problem Solving	Defining a problem, analyzing, creating mental images, generating possible solutions, anticipating, predicting outcomes, evaluating

(Continued)

Table 6.1 *(Continued)*

| Self-Regulation | Inhibitory Control | Attending to a person or activity, focusing, concentrating, thinking before acting, initiating a task, persisting in a task, maintaining social appropriateness |
| | Self-Awareness | Self-assessing, overcoming temptation, monitoring performance, reflecting on goals, managing conflicting thoughts |

For students, having a powerful, CCSS-aligned textbook might be nice; having a masterful teacher who knows how to differentiate instruction and ensure that activities are a cognitive match for students is important. However, a student who lacks the skills listed in Table 6.1 will most likely not be able to take advantage of those factors. And while cognitive ability to construct meaning (covered in chapter 4) is important, it is inextricably linked to executive function.

"In practice, these [executive function] skills support the process (i.e., the *how*) of learning—focusing, remembering, planning—that enables children to effectively and efficiently master the *content* (i.e., the *what*) of learning—reading, writing, computation" (Center on the Developing Child at Harvard University, 2011, p. 5). Attention to these skills does not mean teachers have to teach more; it means they have to think differently about how they teach academic content, and embed executive function into the learning process. First, let's delve more deeply into how the brain handles executive function.

The Prefrontal Cortex

Behind your forehead, at the forefront of your brain, lies a thick outer layer of the frontal lobe known as the prefrontal cortex. This area of the brain handles all of the abilities listed in Table 6.1, which makes it a critically important part of the brain for success in school. The discovery of the importance of the prefrontal cortex is relatively new in the field of education, with Goldman-Rakic's breakthroughs in studying this area of the brain—previously thought inaccessible—occurring in the 1970s. Only recently has the prefrontal cortex received the attention it is due.

The prefrontal cortex does not fully develop in a healthy human being until about the age of 25. This speaks to why so many high school and college students exhibit seemingly poor judgment in terms of decisions related to drugs, sex, alcohol, and social interactions. The prefrontal cortex experiences a significant growth spurt between the ages of three and five. During this time, children are solidifying their ability to reason, respond to cause-

and-effect situations, plan, monitor their behavior, and so forth. Growth then slows but steadily increases through about age 25, after which time it begins to decline steadily throughout the rest of one's life. Dysfunction of the prefrontal cortex is associated with attention deficit hyperactivity disorder (ADHD), Parkinson's disease, Alzheimer's disease, and dementia. It is the degeneration of the prefrontal cortex that leads to age-related dementia. Both stress and diet (high levels of sugar and wheat) adversely affect the development and maintenance of the prefrontal cortex.

The prefrontal cortex of the female brain is larger than that of the male brain and develops more quickly (Eliot, 2009). These facts, combined with other brain and hormonal differences, can account for why more boys than girls tend to have difficulty in school and are diagnosed with ADHD.

The Effect of Poverty on the Prefrontal Cortex

Schools serving students in high poverty areas often experience poor standardized test results, and their approach is to ratchet up the academic exercises: double the amount of time students spend in math or English language arts class; increase the amount of practice activities students must complete; and provide multiple instructional sessions on key topics. Taking low achievers and giving them additional periods of ELA and math that focus on academic skills, and emphasizing instruction focusing on cognitive skills, will do little to raise achievement. A more effective approach, as Paul Tough (2013) suggests, would be to address executive function deficits, which will lead to increased academic achievement. He studied a middle-school chess team and realized that the way the teacher was making her thinking transparent and teaching her students to analyze and strategize was more about executive function than content.

Interestingly enough, we build executive function skills much more so in the areas of fine, performing, physical, and practical arts—the very areas that schools reduce in favor of academics for struggling learners. Rather than a student engaging in the skills of problem solving, cause-and-effect, self-monitoring, collaboration, and focus required in the process of making a clay pot, we pull students out of the special area classes to offer them more academic help. Imagine if, instead, students were engaged in building a clay pot while measuring the components, calculating surface area and volume, and reflecting on and writing about the process.

In his book *How Children Succeed*, Paul Tough (2013) explores the negative effect of stress on the development of the prefrontal cortex:

> The part of the brain most affected by early stress is the prefrontal
> cortex, which is critical in self-regulatory activities of all kinds,

both emotional and cognitive. As a result, children who grow up in stressful environments generally find it harder to concentrate, harder to sit still, harder to rebound from disappointments, and harder to follow directions. And that has a direct effect on their performance in school.

(Tough, 2013, p. 17)

Researchers have found that chronic stress can actually inhibit the growth of the prefrontal cortex. This could explain the reason why some students do not exhibit the same levels of executive function as their peers.

The human body exhibits a complex response to a stressful situation, known as the "fight or flight" response. Consider that early humans would encounter aggressive animals or other humans and have to decide to fight or flee, in either case, needing a lot of muscle strength. When a person is faced with a stressful situation, the body releases adrenaline and cortisol. Cortisol is a steroid that increases blood sugar levels in the blood, needed for muscles to either fight or flee. It directs the body's resources to the muscles and away from what would be considered less-important functions, such as the immune system, digestion, and the development of the prefrontal cortex. The body, however, cannot distinguish between stress caused by an attacking animal and that caused by listening to your parents agonize over how to pay the bills or buy food.

There appears to be a positive correlation between students who live in high-poverty situations and a lack of executive function. Students who live in high-poverty situations experience chronic stress: tension from parents who are trying to make ends meet, parents who are fighting over money, the need to pack up and move regularly, and so forth. With each stressful event, the body produces cortisol. Chronic levels of cortisol inhibit the growth of the prefrontal cortex, resulting in limited executive function, which then contributes to failure in school situations.

The important realization for teachers is that the lack of well-developed executive function may have physiological roots and not be the result of poor parenting, laziness, or lack of caring. If a student walked into a classroom with a broken arm in a sling, the teacher would most likely take steps to accommodate this physical handicap. The same should be true for students who lack executive function. One teacher shared that she would never think of saying to a blind student, "look harder!" and that she now realizes that telling a student with low executive function to try harder makes little sense. In fact, it may be disrespectful. The student is left confused and deflated, thinking that he or she *is* trying harder. Eventually, the student exhibits what appears to be laziness and a lack of motivation, when the behavior is caused by insufficient development of the prefrontal cortex.

The Executive Function—Standards Connection

Return to Table 6.1 and consider just the first three of the fourth-grade ELA standards for reading informational text:

Refer to details and examples in a text when explaining what the text says explicitly and when drawing inferences from the text.

Determine the main idea of a text and explain how it is supported by key details; summarize the text.

Explain events, procedures, ideas, or concepts in a historical, scientific, or technical text, including what happened and why, based on specific information in the text.

Accomplishing these three standards requires storing and manipulating information, remembering details, holding onto information while considering other information, identifying cause-and-effect relationships, categorizing information, catching and correcting errors, analyzing, evaluating, concentrating, working toward a goal, organizing thoughts and actions, considering future consequences in light of current action, attending to an activity, persisting in a task, and more. Students will not be able to achieve these standards without sufficient executive function. You will reach the same conclusion when reading any grade level standards within any ELA strand.

Looking at the math standards, again consider just three of the fourth-grade standards for Operations and Algebraic Thinking:

Interpret a multiplication equation as a comparison, e.g., interpret $35 = 5 \times 7$ as a statement that 35 is 5 times as many as 7 and 7 times as many as 5. Represent verbal statements of multiplicative comparisons as multiplication equations.

> Multiply or divide to solve word problems involving multiplicative comparison, e.g., by using drawings and equations with a symbol for the unknown number to represent the problem, distinguishing multiplicative comparison from additive comparison.

> Solve multistep word problems posed with whole numbers and having whole-number answers using the four operations, including problems in which remainders must be interpreted. Represent these problems using equations with a letter standing for the unknown quantity. Assess the reasonableness of answers using mental computation and estimation strategies including rounding.

These three standards require many of the skills listed in Table 6.1; students will not be able to achieve the level of understanding and application demanded here without sufficient executive function. Organizational and self-regulatory functions are critical to higher-order thinking and success in school, particularly when the emphasis is on more than mere procedural automaticity. Today's classrooms must teach not only the *what* of the standards, but include the *how* of building executive function in the midst of teaching content.

Preparing Students for College, Career, and Life

At the turn of the 21st century, educators began talking about the skills needed to thrive in this new, technology-rich, global society. The Partnership for 21st Century Skills identifies the "four C's": communication, collaboration, critical thinking, and creativity and innovation. Executive function plays a key role in achieving each of the four C's. Without cognitive flexibility, working memory, planning, reasoning, problem solving, inhibitory control, and self-awareness, you won't effectively communicate, collaborate, think critically, and create and innovate.

The ELA CCSS begin with a description of students who are college- and career-ready. Those characteristics all require executive function. Consider the description of the first characteristic, demonstrating independence: "Students are able independently to discern a speaker's key points, request clarification, and ask relevant questions . . . they become self-directed learners, effectively seeking out and using resources to assist them, including teachers, peers, and print and digital reference material."

The CCSS math practice standards read like an executive function primer:

Students should be able to make sense of problems and persevere in solving them; reason abstractly and quantitatively, construct viable arguments and critique the reasoning of others, model with mathematics, use appropriate tools strategically, attend to precision, look for and make use of structure, and look for and express regularity in repeated reasoning.

Teaching Executive Function

The silver lining here is that the prefrontal cortex can be stimulated to develop. This is good news considering that students will not reach the levels of understanding and application required of the CCSS without strong executive function skills. From a physiological standpoint, exercise is important for reversing the adverse effects of stress and diet on the prefrontal cortex and should be an integral part of any school program. The following sections, however, offer a few strategies for actively teaching executive function in the classroom, using the seven components outlined in Table 6.1.

Cognitive Flexibility

Cognitive flexibility involves shifting focus from one event to another, changing perspective, seeing multiple sides to a situation, being open to others' points of view, being creative, catching and correcting errors, and thinking about multiple concepts simultaneously. It can be enhanced through the questions teachers ask about perspective, comparisons, and accuracy (addressed further in chapter 8). Whether referring to curricular content or something a student shares about life outside of school, the teacher can ask students to share what the other person or people listening to the story might have been thinking or feeling, and ask them to compare and contrast. For example, if a student said his team won a baseball game last night, the teacher can ask if he can remember the last time they won a game or the last time they lost a game. How did it feel? What was different about this time? How does he think the other team felt? What was different about how the losing team played? Rather than anxiously awaiting the end of the story so the class can get back to the curriculum, teachers can capitalize on these personal-story moments to build cognitive flexibility. Imagine starting class with a moment where students in pairs share an experience of interest to them and ask one another questions related to perspectives, comparisons, error correction, etc. Table 6.2 offers a table of questions to guide their thinking. These are some of the types of questions that build cognitive flexibility; you could use others as well. Teachers can then build to the point where students are sharing experiences related to classroom

Table 6.2   Support for Cognitive Flexibility

Share Your Experience

Directions: Work with a partner. One person should share a short story of an experience outside of school that involved more than one person. It could be about sports, a musical event, a performance, a vacation, etc. After the story, both partners work to discuss and fill out the chart below. Then the other partner should share a story and do the same.

Who were the main "characters" in the story?	
Did everyone in the story share the same perspective or did anyone feel or think differently from the storyteller?	
If someone did feel or think differently, why do you think that person thought or felt differently?	
What might have happened that would have made the story turn out differently?	
What did the storyteller learn from the experience?	
What would the storyteller do differently next time?	

activities, such as: Share what happened when your group conducted that science experiment; share what happened during the Battle of Yorktown; share your interpretation of the painting; and so forth.

From a curricular perspective, certain aspects of learning activities enhance cognitive flexibility. The teacher can ask students to view a situation from multiple perspectives. A popular follower to the story book *Little Red Riding Hood* had the story told from the perspective of the wolf. These two accounts, and other similar sets of books told from different perspectives, can be used to have students compare and contrast the accounts. A fourth-grade teacher asked students to write articles for a newspaper that might have been published during the Civil War, with one newspaper being a publication from the north, one being from the south, one being from the slaves, and so forth. Debates in which students are asked to prepare not only their argument but counterarguments to what they feel the opposition will present help students build cognitive flexibility. Venn diagrams can be used to have students see multiple sides to a situation, with each circle representing a perspective and the overlap areas of agreement among the perspectives.

Working Memory

Working memory refers to the ability to hold two or more pieces of information in memory at the same time so that you can work with them. Suppose someone says to you, "The luggage you wanted that was $150 retail is on sale for 20% off and I have a $15 coupon you can use." In order for you to mentally calculate that the luggage will cost you $105, in addition to math skills, you need working memory. You have to be able to work with the $150 and 20%, and, after calculating the discount, you have to recall the amount of the coupon. As you get older and your prefrontal cortex deteriorates, you will find yourself saying, "And how much was the coupon again?" Students, however, should have strong working memory, given their potential for prefrontal cortex development.

There are two types of working memory: auditory and visual. Teachers can build their students' working memory in a variety of ways. When providing learning activities that include directions, teachers can train students to read the directions, then look away from the paper and tell a partner what the directions say to do. Teachers can engage students in games such as *Concentration* that require them to remember words or terms they see that are uncovered, and then hidden again as they attempt to match terms to terms or definitions. Some online quiz games offer you the opportunity to design content-related games of this style. Teachers can record short (30- to 60-second) podcasts on curricular topics and have students take a quiz on key information. Then the students should listen again to assess their memory, and then correct the quiz using an answer key. The goal is, obviously, to build to a point where students listen to a podcast and score 100% every time.

Planning

Cognitive planning refers to the process of establishing a set of steps to achieve a goal. This can take place abstractly, as in deciding upon the next chess move, or concretely, as in developing a set of steps to complete a project. Depending on the executive function strength of the students, teachers may begin by detailing steps to complete a project. For example: "To research your chosen state to create a tour, first you must complete a set of note cards from three different sources; then you must create a graphic organizer of the information you gathered. To create a set of note cards, first you must identify a valid source for information; then you must look for information on your state that has to do with places to stop that highlight history, geography, or geology. . . ." Checklists and organizers will help students to see the steps. Over time, students should create their own checklists, thinking through an assignment to determine what steps they need to take to accomplish it.

In student-centered, differentiated classrooms, teachers can have students create schedules for how they will complete activities. Students should identify each activity along with a clear start and end time, rather than just checking off activities as they complete them. The start and end time focuses students on a temporal goal as well as a curricular goal. At the end of a day or week, students can reflect on their schedule and how well they followed it. Why did an activity take longer than planned? Why did an activity take less time than planned? What could students have done differently to be more productive? These questions relate to executive function.

Abstract cognitive planning can be enhanced through playing games of strategy. Teachers of elementary-level students can provide them time to play checkers, chess, and other similar games. They can provide them with a "move chart" that requires them to think through why they chose that particular move and what the outcome was when their opponent took a turn: Did the move turn out as planned or did they encounter a surprise? Older students can engage in content-related simulations—again, charting out a move and reflecting on the outcome.

When having students solve multi-step math problems, balancing chemical equations, crafting arguments, and other similar multi-step challenges, teachers should have students first write down the steps they will take, forcing them to plan their approach. Over time, as executive function builds, that step can be eliminated.

Reasoning

Reasoning allows you to move beyond the data to use them in ways that will help you in life. You apply reasoning when you decide the best approach to take or decision to make; essentially, you solidify your *reason* for doing so. You must consider fact from opinion; evaluate options, thus taking into account cause-and-effect relationships; consider similar situations you've experienced; hypothesize; deduce; and infer.

At a beginning level of reasoning, teachers can ask students to identify relevant information in a paragraph of informational text or math word problems; this task requires reasoning skills. They can ask students to analyze analogies, which requires reasoning skills. Teachers can help students identify the difference between reason and emotion; they can build a classroom culture in which students must justify their decisions with evidence and logic.

Reasoning typically involves a set of processes. Reasoning through when to complete one's homework would involve taking into account other commitments, other desired activities, one's mental state after accomplishing those, and so forth, to determine if the best time to complete homework would be right at the end of the school day or later in the evening. Teachers can simply ask students to justify their choice of when to complete their homework to get the reasoning process going. As students engage in making choices in class, once again, teachers can ask them to justify their choices in order to focus on reasoning skills. Reasoning can also be partnered with planning when engaging students in playing games of strategy, asking them to explain their reasoning for a particular sequence of moves.

In the content areas, opportunities to reason abound. Simple lists of numbers or shapes in which the student has to determine the pattern, and thus the next item, build logical reasoning skills. Reasoning skills are necessary when developing an experiment around plant growth and sharing the reasoning related to the hypothesis; considering a current event and similar events in history to reason how to address the current situation; deciding if it is reasonable to build a resort in a desert; sharing why a character behaved in a particular way in a novel; explaining how to solve a math problem; etc. Often, well-written essential questions provide the backdrop for reasoning. Graphic organizers can help students organize their thoughts. Table 6.3 offers a few simple tables for helping students reason through a situation.

Table 6.3   Support for Reasoning

Observations and Details	Patterns	Conclusion

I Know This . . .	Which Means . . .	Which Means . . .

My Decision Is This . . .	Based On . . .

Problem Solving

Problem solving is a more complex executive function that depends upon the others. In the course of generating problem solutions, for example, you must rely on reasoning, planning, working memory, and cognitive flexibility. Math problems tend to be closed-ended in that there is one right answer. Real-world problems from other subject areas tend to be open-ended. Figuring out how much paint to buy to cover a room with known dimensions is a closed-ended problem; deciding on a plan to build a habitat for a cloned dinosaur is an open-ended problem. Solving a closed-ended problem involves:

1. Defining the problem—Students should describe the problem to ensure they are clear on what they have to solve.

2. Gathering data—Students should determine the data that are available to them that relates to the problem.

3. Choosing an approach—Different problems require different approaches. Some popular approaches are to represent the problem through drawings or manipulatives; make a calculated guess, perhaps using patterns; act out the problem; identify a known algorithm for the situation; or draw on past, similar problems.

4. Implementing the approach—At this point, students should attempt to solve the problem.

5. Checking for accuracy—Students now replay the problem with the solution to ensure that they are correct.

Solving an open-ended problem involves:

1. Defining the problem—Students should describe the problem to ensure they are clear on what they have to solve.

2. Generating questions related to the problem—Students should generate a series of questions on the topic that will help them develop a solution.

3. Gathering data to answer the questions—Students should seek out the answers to questions, which might raise additional questions to be answered.

4. Brainstorming possible solutions.

5. Gathering data to determine the feasibility of the solution, including considering possible unintended consequences.

6. Implementing the solution.

7. Evaluating the success of the solution.

8. Returning to a prior step, if necessary.

Teachers should engage students in problem solving related to content on a regular basis, beginning with easier problems. For example, a science teacher might ask, "When planting flower seeds, approximately 90% germinate; if you plant 68 seeds, how many plants can you expect?" For an open-ended problem, the teacher might ask, "Given the different needs and sizes of plants, how would you design a six-foot by ten-foot garden for the front of a school in Pasco County, Florida?" The above steps can be converted into tables for students to follow as they build their problem-solving skills.

Inhibitory Control

Inhibitory control refers to managing one's tendency to give into distractions or desires. It covers a wide variety of distinct skills, most of which students develop prior to attending school. For students who are unable to attend to a person, the teacher can begin with activities in which the student is working solely with one other person, perhaps engaging in a conversation where each speaker begins a response by simply repeating what the other speaker said. So the conversation might sound like this:

Speaker 1: I really like ice cream.
Speaker 2: You like ice cream. I like cookies more.
Speaker 1: You like cookies. My favorite cookie is chocolate chip.
Speaker 2: Your favorite cookie is chocolate chip; mine is peanut butter.

Short conversations like this, either about personal likes or events or about subject area content, can build students' ability to attend to another person.

For students who have difficulty attending to a task, the teacher might offer short goals, such as working uninterrupted for five minutes, after which time the teacher would commend the student and perhaps initial a card to indicate success. After enough success at one level, the next goal can be a longer period of time, such as ten minutes. Teachers should avoid having the student track time at first, as the tracking itself can distract the student from the activity.

For students who have difficulty persisting in a task, a graphic reflection sheet can help (see Table 6.4). Teachers can help students identify the

Table 6.4   Support for Task Persistence

When I want to give up . . .

I Feel . . .	Because . . .	But I Will Try To . . .
☐ Frustrated		
☐ Angry		
☐ Confused		
☐ Lost		
☐ _____		
☐		

adjectives in the first column to describe how they typically feel when they want to give up. Having them acknowledge the feeling and set a goal to continue on, perhaps making some adjustment, will build the skill of task persistence. Students may decide to keep trying a little longer, ask a colleague for help, ask the teacher for help, look for information online, etc.

Refer to Table 6.1 to see the various components of inhibitory control. Teachers can focus on each component to help students build strength in these areas through short-term, attainable goals, graphic organizers or checklists, repetition, and positive feedback.

Self-Awareness

Self-awareness involves recognizing your strengths, actions, and accomplishments in light of goals and responsibilities. For students with significant deficits in executive function, teachers can work with each student to set a short-term academic goal and write it on a card to keep on the student's desk. The teacher and student can check in at intervals to assess progress.

At a more sophisticated level, teachers can offer students opportunities to set and reflect on goals through the use of analytic rubrics. Teachers can offer students a rubric that provides academic expectations and require them (assisting where needed) to read through the rubric and underline everything they need to learn. This will focus students on academic expectations while building executive function. The subtle addition of a rubric that lays out clearly articulated expectations, along with the teacher's use of it as a continual tool of student self-reflection, will build executive function by having students focus, set goals, self-assess, and monitor performance. The rubric should be available at all times so that the teacher can facilitate by asking students where they are on the rubric and what their plan is for moving to the next level.

The Great Student Rubric

Teachers can help all students build executive function by designing a rubric for work habits; Table 6.5 offers an example. Teachers should design such rubrics to match age-appropriate expectations. Teachers can help students who have significantly weak executive function by offering them just one row of the rubric to attend to at a time.

When students simply sit in their seats and attend to a teacher's lesson, taking notes and making meaning, they are not building executive function; and if their executive function is weak, they are probably not constructing meaning out of the academic content. Those who possess strong executive function are most likely compliant, will take notes, and will construct meaning abstractly, either while in the lesson or at home later when they attempt to make sense of their notes. When students engage in learning while setting goals, self-assessing, making choices, reflecting on progress, working with a partner, and so forth, they are building executive function and making meaning. A Great Student rubric can address executive function in any content-area classroom, ensuring that students are building the skills they need to benefit from the content instruction. As Olympic athlete Wilma Rudolph said, "The potential for greatness lives within each of us." Teachers can help students tap into that greatness by helping them build executive function—the key to academic achievement.

Table 6.5 Great Student Rubric

This rubric will help you become a great student in this class! Read each row and identify your progress. Then set goals to accomplish the next level to the right until you get to *Practitioner* or *Expert*.

	Novice	Apprentice	Practitioner	Expert
Noise Level	moderates voice to match venue with prompting from teacher	moderates voice to match venue at times; requires an occasional reminder from teacher	moderates voice to match venue	moderates voice to match venue; respectfully reminds others to keep voices at a reasonable level
Roles	carries out assigned role with some prompting from teacher and/or peers	carries out chosen or assigned role in a group effectively	works with group members to assign rotating roles (such as Materials Person, Recorder, Timekeeper, Reader) as noted; carries out role effectively	actively contributes to determining necessary roles for a task and assigning them; carries out roles effectively
Work Responsibility	completes work with some teacher prompting regarding deadlines	completes most work to be handed in on time; usually meets team deadlines	completes all work to be handed in on time; always meets deadlines	*all of Practitioner* plus, when finished early, works to improve upon the work handed in
Focus	stays on task with prompting from teacher and/or peers	generally stays on task; catches oneself and gets back on task without teacher or peer prompting	stays on task; reserves off-task conversations for lunch time	*all of Practitioner* plus respectfully reminds others to do the same
Time Management	plans to schedule with significant assistance from teacher	plans schedule with feedback from teacher; reflects on why activities took significantly more or less time than planned	plans schedule well for completing activities; generally completes activities within time limits; makes adjustments as needed without sacrificing performance	*all of Practitioner* plus can explain strategies for effectively planning a schedule to others

Folder Organization	folders organized with work completed on one side and work in progress on the other	folders organized with work completed on one side and work in progress on the other; completed and checked work is removed within a week	folders organized with recently completed work for the teacher to review on one side, work in progress on the other side; support materials are stored elsewhere; completed and checked work is removed immediately	*all of Practitioner* plus places a sheet of questions, where necessary, at the top of the work-in-progress

In Summary

Developing students' executive function means:

♦ Recognizing the critical connection between executive function and academic achievement

♦ Acknowledging that lack of executive function may have physiological roots and treating students as such

♦ Recognizing that executive function is inherent in most of the CCSS

♦ Actively teaching students the skills related to cognitive flexibility, working memory, planning, reasoning, problem solving, inhibitory control, and self-awareness

Chapter 7

The Sixth Insight

Purposeful Instruction Yields Retention

I never teach my pupils, I only attempt to provide the conditions in which they can learn.

—Albert Einstein

Purposeful instruction melds a focus on achievement of the end-goal of each standard with an understanding of the learning needs of an individual student; the process increases the likelihood that students will learn and, more importantly, retain learning. Learning comes from within; it is the point at which one's brain makes the appropriate connections and constructs meaning, then stores the information in long-term memory so that it can later be retrieved and applied. Teachers, then, must be the architects of deliberate and purposeful classroom environments that inspire and support learning retention.

The Learning Hourglass

Learning, in the broadest sense, has three stages: motivation, acquisition, and retention (see Figure 7.1).

Figure 7.1 The Learning Hourglass

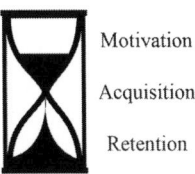

Motivation

Acquisition

Retention

Understanding these stages helps to narrow the focus of purposeful teaching. We are motivated to learn through our environment: Something sparks our interest, gains our attention. Learning typically begins with a question, desire, or need. I may notice a sunflower and wonder what makes it grow. I may see someone play the flute and decide that I want to learn to play. I may be ready to travel to a foreign country and decide I first want to learn the language. The environment is a wonderful motivator for learning; babies demonstrate that continuously through their exploration, curiosity, and questioning. People are motivated by watching others, exploring, observing, reading, viewing, feeling, and so forth. These experiences trigger awareness of knowledge to be learned (Gattegno, 1987–2010).

Once the motivation is in place, the brain narrows the focus. If I want to learn to play the flute, I may begin watching the flautist's posture, finger movements, and mouth in an attempt to model them. I learn one skill at a time. I may mimic the flautist to produce a sound; then I will focus on producing specific notes; then I will focus on louder and softer tones; and so forth. This is the acquisition phase. The reality is that the brain can only cognitively process one piece of information at a time. The brain processes at such speeds that it may appear to be handling more than one piece of information at a time, but it is not. In the acquisition phase of learning, the focus is very narrow.

As people learn skills, concepts, and information, they must retain them. The brain works to create schemas—that is, collections of related experiences and information represented through the strengthening of neural connections. You may see a person and call to mind her name, career, where she lives, her family, and so forth. This is possible because of schemas that are built in your brain that represent the sum total of all of the knowledge you possess. The retention of and building on existing skills, concepts, and content create a personal knowledge base. The larger the knowledge base, the more a person knows and is able to do. Learning for a moment and failing to retain the knowledge won't help people throughout their lives.

If you consider learning as a three-stage process, the CCSS define the bottom of the hourglass, or the retention stage. They define what students should have learned and retained by certain grade levels; and they make the assumption that learning is cumulative, so retaining what was learned in the prior year is essential. Teaching to any goal other than retention falls short of ensuring that students achieve the standards.

The Motivation Factor

All learning begins with motivation, even if it is merely to please the teacher, a parent, or oneself. The best motivation emerges from students' experiences and desires. The CCSS define what students must learn.

Teachers must determine the best way to motivate individual students toward achieving the CCSS. When students possess a felt need to learn (Sulla, 2011), the likelihood of acquisition and retention increases. Problem-based learning (addressed in chapter 3) can be used successfully to build a felt need to learn. The greater the personal connection to the learning, the greater the likelihood of acquisition and retention.

Motivation is strongly linked to retention. The motivation to please the teacher or a parent prompts the student to learn and retain for a period of time, often to achieve a high grade on a test. After that achievement, retention is no longer necessary. Motivation through fear rarely produces lasting results, if it produces even temporary results. Motivation that emerges from the individual leads to higher retention rates. A high school English teacher noted that on any given day, one or more students failed to bring their books to class. He launched a unit, "For the Love of Literature," and allowed students to self-select the books they would read. Students were all reading different novels, and, as such, the teacher had to focus discussion on broad questions. He found that it was rare that a student failed to bring the book to class. The students were motivated because they had a personal connection to the novel they were each reading.

A fifth-grade teacher launched a social studies unit allowing students to consider the time period and the various lenses through which a person could view history (e.g., through commerce, conflict, communication, transportation, politics, etc.). The teacher asked students to identify a non-Google-able problem that included cause-and-effect relationships that existed in this time period and still remains today. Their goal was to find a problem and pose a solution. The teacher reported that students were fully engaged and very serious about finding just the right problems. They were motivated by the responsibility she gave them and the fact that they could study the period of history through a lens that was meaningful to them.

Every standard deserves attention to the motivation factor. Narrowing the focus to determining the motivation for addressing one standard, however, will most likely end up driving students to multiple standards. Consider the ELA standard RL.8.3, which states:

> Analyze how particular lines of dialogue or incidents in a story or drama propel the action, reveal aspects of a character, or provoke a decision.

An eighth-grade English teacher, in having her students read *The Pearl*, chose to focus on the theme of retrogressive characters. She presented her students with the task of comparing and contrasting the fictional main character of the novel with a real-life, modern-day, retrogressive character found among those typically in the news (sports figures, musical artists, politicians, actors, etc.). Students found the challenge particularly motivating, most likely because they were applying the theme from the novel to real-word situations. While it's easy to see how standard RL.8.3 would be addressed through this exercise, it turns out that several other standards across the ELA category were included as well. However, narrowing the focus again to this one standard—the problem-based situation with which the teacher presented her students—produced the motivation for students to tackle the novel, the theme of retrogressive characters, and the standard related to analyzing dialogue and events.

The Acquisition Factor

The human brain is highly focused when acquiring new knowledge, mastering one concept or skill at a time. When a young child watches a bird take flight, she develops an understanding that the flapping of the wings allows the bird to fly; she is not at the same time focusing on the bird's feet. She may in the next second develop an understanding that the bird's feet are extended back during flight; she may soon come to understand that the position of the feet enhances the aerodynamics, allowing the bird to fly more easily. All of these understandings, however, develop one at a time.

The brain also focuses on learning from large to small. The child watches the bird fly, understanding that she herself cannot fly. She then ponders what makes a bird fly and how she and the bird are different. As she continues to explore, she moves to the more detailed level of each concept. Learning to cook a new dish begins with an overall understanding of the dish itself, then deconstructing the dish to the ingredients. *Learning* to cook a new dish does not begin with merely measuring ingredients; *cooking* the dish does.

Acquisition is a personal process. No one can force you to learn. Masterful teachers follow the lead of Einstein, who said, "I never teach my pupils, I only attempt to provide the conditions in which they can learn." The key to teaching the level of understanding and application required by the CCSS is purposefully designing instruction to enable students to pursue personal learning.

Learning Is Hard

Theories on the conditions under which students acquire new knowledge fill volumes; the topic is the focus of continued research on the brain and learning. This is where differentiated learning opportunities come into play. Students need to grapple with new content, explore it, make sense of it, and struggle with it; learning is hard.

> Learning is a process of meaning making, not of knowledge transmission. Humans interact with other humans and with artifacts in the world and naturally and continuously attempt to make sense of those interactions. Meaning making (resolving the dissonance between what we know for sure and what we perceive or what we believe that others know) results from a puzzlement, perturbation, expectation violations, curiosity, or cognitive dissonance. Making meaning from phenomena and experiences involves dissonance between what we know and what we want or need to know.
>
> (Jonassen & Land, 2012, p. ix)

Cognitive dissonance is a psychological state of discomfort that occurs when a gap exists between what one knows and what one needs to learn. Some level of cognitive dissonance must exist in order for learning to take place; thus, learning does not come without some level of discomfort. Students, therefore, are more likely to persevere through the learning struggle if they are well motivated.

Additionally, students will be more likely to succeed at learning when they are grappling, having encountered a challenge, and have some place to turn for help. That help could come from a printed how-to sheet, a peer, a website, a podcast, a reference book, or a teacher. A fifth-grade teacher had her students research how to spend the $15,000 fund the school had to replenish the foliage that was destroyed around the school during a recent construction project. As her students researched indigenous plants and created their budgets, one student approached the teacher, perplexed because she could not figure out how to subtract $478.58 from $15,000 because she had all these extra numbers. She was experiencing cognitive dissonance, a requirement for true learning. The teacher was able to help her see that she needed to include a decimal point and two zeros in the larger number so that they could line up. The student experienced an "aha" moment she will no doubt remember when faced with other similar situations.

It is important to ensure that when students encounter these learning struggles that cause them to grapple, they have available to them activities and resources that are well-suited for their dominant learning modalities and their cognitive levels. Most teachers learn in college that it is important to provide auditory, visual, and tactile/kinesthetic learning activities to students to increase the likelihood of acquisition of new knowledge. Borrowing from Lev Vygotsky's work, the likelihood of acquisition is also increased when providing learning experiences to students matched to their zone of proximal development. Students who understand the concept of a noun are ready to learn verbs or adjectives; they are not ready to learn passive voice. Students who understand prepositional phrases most likely do not need a lesson in nouns. Differentiation must go beyond learning modalities and accept that not all students are ready to tackle the same content at the same time.

Additionally, students will have interaction preferences. Some prefer to hear from the teacher; some prefer to learn from their peers; some prefer to seek out the answer online or through books. The key is to provide for the "leveling up" (chapter 4) and supports that allow students to work through their challenges successfully so they are motivated to follow each achievement with a new quest. A well-motivated student, given a variety of opportunities to learn that match learning modality and cognitive readiness, will be more likely to achieve knowledge acquisition.

The Retention Factor

The goal of learning is long-term retention—understanding, remembering, and being able to apply knowledge at a future time. The common teaching practice of reviewing before a test presumes that students have not retained the learning; the goal of teaching was not retention. If students can't recall information "learned" a week ago, how will they recall it a year from now? This is the reason that teachers often feel their colleagues at the prior grade level failed to teach content. In reality, the teachers most likely did teach it. The question is whether or not students learned and retained it.

David Kolb (1984) developed his experiential learning theory from the perspective of internal cognitive processes that lead to long-term retention. Figure 7.2 depicts four stages that lead to learning.

Figure 7.2   Kolb's Four Stages of Learning

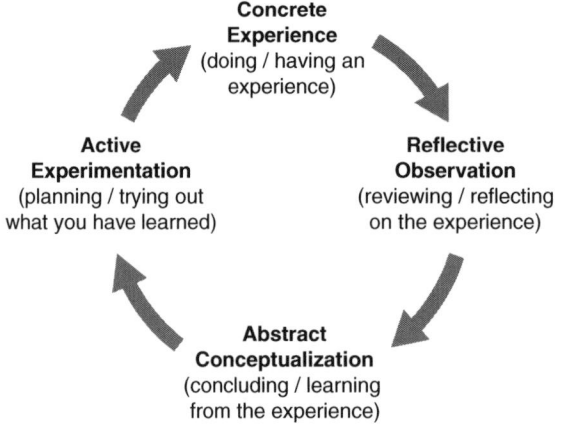

The student engages in a concrete experience, followed by observation and reflection on that experience, which leads to repeated analysis and conclusions resulting in abstract conceptualization, followed by active experimentation applying learning to new situations. Consider the story of the fifth-grader attempting to subtract money. She experienced the problem situation and sought out the teacher, continuing the concrete experience phase while engaging with the teacher in the problem. She then observed the solution to the dilemma and reflected on that. She then conceptualized the role of the decimal point and trailing zeros in subtraction of money. Finally, she returned to her group to share her learning, and continued to subtract money successfully, applying the learning to new situations.

Students are more likely to retain learning when they are motivated through a felt need to learn, when they have a personal connection and motivation to the content. Additionally, they are more likely to retain learning when they build acquisition through experiences that cause them to use information and construct meaning through abstract conceptualization. If I learn a skill, concept, or piece of information that makes sense and has meaning because I have connected it to a greater context, I will retain it (Sousa, 2005). Alternatively, if I learn a skill, concept, or piece of information simply because the teacher presented it today, I may retain it only long enough to make the teacher, myself, and/or my parents happy through the completion of an assignment or test.

Students are more likely to retain learning when they encounter and utilize the knowledge repeatedly, over time. This is highlighted in the assigning of math homework. Mathematics is a clear example of a subject in which a student must grapple with a concrete skill and then create conceptual abstractions to build understanding and retain the learning. It is important for students to leave school and return to the skill through the homework assignment hours later. This allows them to retrieve the information from their brain or notes and continue the conceptualization process. When teachers allow students to finish their homework in school, they run the risk of students merely following a procedure rather than constructing knowledge. One of the early tests of learning new content is if you can walk away from it and later return to it with success.

Likewise, it is important to return to that learning over time, across the course and across the years. The notion that once a topic is covered, it's time to move on to another topic—thus assuming the first is now etched in memory—is a flawed one. Retention is increased when students continue to make connections to content and utilize it in a variety of situations. Thus, learning environments that build on prior knowledge and cause students to return to knowledge previously learned increase the likelihood of long-term retention.

The Shift Away From Whole-Class Information Delivery

More and more teachers are realizing that while whole-class instruction can give them a sense of comfort in that they covered the curriculum, it is not the most effective way to teach. Harvard professor Eric Mazur found that in spite of his powerful lectures, his physics students were not grasping the basic concepts of physics, although they could perform well on tests of procedural automaticity. He was inspired by the findings of David Hestenes, who stumbled upon this negative correlation of lecture to learning:

> The students had improved at handling equations and formulas, he explains, but when it came to understanding 'what the real meanings of these things are, they basically reverted to Aristotelian logic—thousands of years back.' For example, they could recite Newton's Third Law and apply it to numerical problems, but when asked about a real-world event like a collision between a heavy truck and a light car, many firmly declared that the heavy truck exerts a larger force. (Actually, an object's weight is irrelevant to the force exerted.)
>
> (Lambert, 2012, p. 1)

Mazur went on to study his own students and found, to his dismay, the same results. He then changed his mode of teaching to actively engage students in learning, becoming their resource and guide.

Actively engaging students in constructing knowledge requires a more student-centered approach to instruction, one in which the teacher moves out of the role of whole-class information deliverer. The challenge is, if the teacher is not presenting skills and concepts, how the children will learn new content. Certainly, understanding will come from engaging with content, but what about the foundational skills through which to engage in the first place? The question is not the value of direct instruction; it is more of the place in time where the instruction takes place, and how. Any form of direct instruction prior to motivation may fall short of the goal of learning. Engaging students in solving authentic, open-ended problems will motivate them and produce a felt-need to learn concepts and skills. While working on solution finding, students will encounter situations for which they do not have the necessary skill or concept. They may grapple with the situation momentarily, which will produce a felt need for them to learn. At that moment, direct instruction is a powerful method of ensuring learning. Just at the point that students need to know, finding the answers they seek will raise the likelihood of retention. However, the whole class will not reach the same point of felt need at the same time. That is the shortcoming of the whole-class lesson.

In a student-centered environment, the teacher needs to ensure that, at the point of felt need, students have a variety of venues through which to receive direct instruction. These can include a one-on-one session with the teacher, a small-group lesson by the teacher, a printed how-to sheet, a podcast or video, a peer expert, a textbook, a learning center, an interactive website, an app, and so forth. With the move out of the front of the classroom comes the responsibility to provide students with ample opportunities to learn. Allowing students to work on their own with little instruction, assuming they will discover the answers or teach themselves, will most likely not lead to success.

Learning Activities vs. Practice Activities

Given that not all students are ready to learn skills at the same time, teachers are attempting to reduce the amount of whole-class instruction they offer, opting instead to actively engage students in more differentiated activities. When teachers provide whole-class skill instruction, they typically follow it with practice activities—those that carry the assumption students have the information needed to accurately complete them. Eliminating the whole-class lesson, however, does not eliminate the need for instruction. Assigning what are essentially practice activities without any instruction can cause students to be confused and feel like they are teaching themselves. With the move out of the front of the room comes the need to design "learning activities": activities that focus on providing learning opportunities for students to acquire new concepts or skills. While teachers can still provide small-group and one-on-one direct instruction, students should also engage in learning activities independent from the teacher in order to take greater responsibility for their own learning.

Learning activities have three components: a specific content focus, directions, and feedback. The content should be limited to a particular skill or concept, such as calculating the perimeter of a rectangle, conjugating regular -ar ending verbs in Spanish, the concept of the conservation of mass, and so on. This way, the student's brain can focus on a specific understanding and not get confused by too broad a focus.

Directions provide direct instruction. Learning activities are not intended to engage students in discovery learning; they are intended to offer an alternative to the whole-class, teacher-directed lesson and to build greater student responsibility for learning. The directions may be more open-ended, such as, "See how many figures you can create with the geometric pieces"; or they may be more structured, such as, "Fill a beaker with a cup of cold water."

The feedback might be very specific and prefabricated, such as that provided by an answer key, or it might be offered through evidence of successful completion. As an example of the latter, a learning activity might teach a student how to construct a flat template to make a cube. As the student follows the directions to draw the template and fold and glue the sides, a three-dimensional cube emerges. The existence of the cube is feedback enough.

There are four types of learning activities (see Table 7.1). It is appropriate for students to engage in exploration of concepts and skills. As an introductory activity, students might be offered a collection of rocks and minerals to observe, categorize, and explore in an attempt to raise questions and draw conclusions, prior to any other instruction. This would be an example of an "Exploration Without Feedback" learning activity. An activity in which students are instructed to create three piles of rocks based on similarity of look and feel, accompanied with an answer key pointing

Table 7.1   Four Types of Learning Activities

Type of Learning Activity	Examples
Exploration Without Feedback—The student engages in an open-ended introductory exploration of a concept or skill, making connections, generating questions, testing hypotheses, and drawing conclusions.	Learning Center Manipulatives Experiments Computer Simulations Computer Apps
Exploration With Feedback—The student engages in a structured introductory exploration with feedback, based on specific anticipated outcomes.	Learning Center Computer Apps
Direct Instruction With Passive Student Participation—The student watches or listens to a visual, auditory, or text-based explanation or set of steps to follow to build understanding of a concept or skill.	Podcast Screencast Videocast Text
Direct Instruction With Active Student Participation—The student follows a set of steps to build understanding of a concept or skill, with feedback to self-correct.	How-To Sheet Interactive Website or App Learning Center Podcast Screencast Videocast

out igneous, sedimentary, and metamorphic rocks, would be an example of an "Exploration With Feedback" learning activity. The teacher might provide a video of a geologist conducting specific tests to identify minerals through their color, streak, transparency, luster, etc. This would be an example of a "Direct Instruction With Passive Student Participation" learning activity. A how-to sheet in which the student follows directions to conduct a series of tests and attempts to identify minerals, accompanied by an answer key for confirmation, would be an example of a "Direct Instruction With Active Student Participation" learning activity. It is important to provide students with learning activities and, more specifically, a variety of types of learning activities.

Practice activities presume some level of learning has already taken place. Once students have been introduced to the skill of weighing objects, they can weigh many objects and fill in charts. Once they've been introduced to identifying the plot line in a short story, they can draw out the plot line for each short story they read and even design a plot line for a story they will write.

Your Turn
Applying the Learning Hourglass to Your Standards

Select one of the CCSS with which you've been working in this book. You've already distinguished the end from the means. Focusing on that end goal or essence of the standard, begin with motivation: What scenario can you present to your students that will provide the motivation to learn? Then move on to acquisition. Think of three students in your class: an average student, a gifted student, and a struggling student. Brainstorm the types of instructional activities each of them would need to acquire the knowledge required by the standard you chose. Finally, consider retention: What about your learning environment will connect your students to this content in a way that will yield retention?

Your Turn
Brainstorming Learning Activities

Select a specific curricular skill or concept and brainstorm four types of learning activities to support student learning. Use Table 7.2 as a template for your answers.

Table 7.2 Learning Activities Template

Skill or Concept	
Exploration Without Feedback	
Exploration With Feedback	
Direct Instruction With Passive Student Participation	
Direct Instruction With Active Student Participation	

In Summary

Purposeful instruction means that:

♦ Learning, in the broadest sense, has three stages: motivation, acquisition, and retention

♦ Motivation is strongly linked to retention

♦ The brain processes one piece of information at a time; thus, instruction for acquisition should be narrowly focused

♦ Cognitive dissonance is the gap that exists between what one knows and what one needs to learn, and it is an important condition for learning; thus, learning is hard

♦ Learning is a four-stage process moving from concrete experience to reflective observation to abstract conceptualization to active experimentation

♦ Retention is increased through personal connection and repeated interaction with content

♦ As teachers move away from whole-class instruction, they must add learning activities to their repertoire

♦ Learning activities offer a specific concept or skill focus, directions, and feedback

♦ The four types of learning activities are Exploration Without Feedback, Exploration With Feedback, Direct Instruction With Passive Student Participation, and Direct Instruction With Active Student Participation

Chapter 8

The Seventh Insight

CCSS Achievement Relies on Teacher Facilitation

Education is the kindling of a flame, not the filling of a vessel.

—Socrates

There are moments in school that we all remember when we had a meaningful interaction with a teacher over a topic, assignment, or project. It may have been when a teacher commended us on overcoming a difficult challenge; it may have been a debate in which we attempted to argue our point with our teacher; it may have been a story from our teachers' past that resonated with us. The words and actions of teachers can build up and tear down students. Teachers are a powerful influence in any classroom, making the ways in which they facilitate learning even more important.

The CCSS require students to grapple with skills and concepts to build understanding; learning is hard. The support, suggestion, and inspiration of a masterful teacher can be just what students need to push through to success. The level of thinking and problem solving required by the CCSS moves the teacher from whole-class information dissemination to learning facilitation. At the center of this shift is a belief that it's not enough for teachers to merely present content; they must masterfully facilitate the learning process so that each student achieves success.

The teacher becomes an architect of the learning environment, designing for retention. As students engage in the learning process, the teacher shifts to a masterful facilitator of learning. The first step to becoming a facilitator is to design a learning environment that warrants facilitation. This typically includes having students engaged in activities independently, in pairs, or in small groups. It should include differentiated activities so that not all students are engaged in the same activity at the same time.

Some activities require greater teacher involvement than others. For example, information searches on the Internet, independent reading, journal writing, and watching a podcast are low-teacher-involvement activities. The teacher may check in and ensure students are appropriately progressing, but there is not much need for further interaction in the moment. High-teacher-involvement activities are those in which the student will benefit from the teacher's interaction, such as in designing experiments, discussing a novel, solving a math problem, making a perspective drawing, etc. It is best if the students can be engaged in a mix of low-teacher-involvement and high-teacher-involvement activities in order for the teacher to offer adequate attention to those who need it without feeling stretched too thin.

Once the activities are in place and students are engaged in learning, the teacher becomes an active facilitator. Teachers must sit with, meet with, and interact with students constantly. The teacher's desk is no place to find a teacher when students are in the room. In the role of facilitator, the teacher performs eleven distinctly different functions:

1. Challenge
2. Observe
3. Suggest
4. Instruct
5. Guide
6. Encourage
7. Celebrate
8. Connect
9. Question
10. Glean
11. Design

Challenge

At times, teachers should provide students with challenges that cause them to grapple with content. While this can come in the form of an overarching problem-based task, it can also come in the form of a smaller challenge. For example, a high-school calculus teacher explains to her students that she likes her coffee hot, but with cream. She shares how long it takes her to drive to school and asks her students if they think her coffee would remain hotter if she waited to put the creamers in until after she arrives at school or if she had the cream added at the time of her coffee purchase. This challenge motivates students to attempt to find the answer. A first-grade teacher asks her students to select three books and, from just looking at and reading the covers, identify what they think each book might be about. A fourth-grade teacher asks his students to create a new trail mix from a variety of ingredients, calculating a new nutrition label. All of these challenges set students' minds in motion.

Sometimes the challenge comes in the beginning of a unit of study or set of activities, as just presented; sometimes it comes in the midst of the instruction. A computer teacher has a student write the program code to draw a house with a roof, door, and windows; the teacher then asks if the student can add a chimney. This task requires slightly more sophisticated coding (a "leveling up," as introduced in chapter 3) and challenges the student to attempt to figure it out. A student writes a letter to a company making suggestions for a new product; the teacher asks how the student might ensure the company will write back, challenging the student to consider the writing style, substance, and closing. Teachers facilitate learning by providing big and small challenges that motivate their students to pursue further learning.

Observe

Once students are working, teachers as facilitators begin by simply observing. At times, teachers can visually scan the room to get a sense of the overall classroom activity. Are all students seemingly engaged? Do any look confused, frustrated, or off task? Is there a productive noise in the room, indicating that students are talking about content with one another? Teachers may drift, moving around the room, intrigued to follow a spoken comment or observed behavior, taking in the action.

The teacher should then sit next to a student or group and observe them in action, taking care not to join the discussion too quickly. Teachers must avoid the temptation to start giving out answers and guidance prematurely. Students should be given some time to engage in the current activity, perhaps struggle a little, but not to a level of frustration.

Teachers can observe how students respond in challenging situations. Do they persist in a task? Are they resourceful, seeking out assistance from materials and other people? Are their requests of others specifically targeted to a skill or concept or simply a cry for help? Do they mind being interrupted in the midst of a challenge? Do they prefer to work alone or collaboratively?

Observing students in the midst of a challenge provides teachers with a good deal of information about the students' learning preferences, executive function, and resourcefulness. From there, they can decide which type of facilitation role to utilize next: suggest, instruct, guide, encourage, celebrate, connect, or question.

Suggest

At times, teachers should offer suggestions. This is important if a student seems somewhat frustrated, in which case asking questions to lead the student to arrive at a solution might exacerbate the situation. Instead, teachers offer suggestions that can lead the student closer to answers. For example, if a student is writing a poem and having a difficult time finding an appropriate rhyming word—but guiding the student to a resource to find possible rhyming words might prove to be too frustrating—the teacher can offer a few possible rhyming words to ease the tension and allow the student to have some level of success before moving on to the next challenge. Teachers facilitate learning by making suggestions at appropriate times.

Instruct

At times, teachers should provide students with direct instruction in concepts or skills. If a student is working on a problem but struggling with calculating the perimeter of a rectangle, the teacher can use the opportunity to offer a quick lesson. If a primary student is writing a letter and forgets how to write a capital B, the teacher can point to a letter chart and ask the student what she remembers about writing the letter B, but then model how to construct the letter for the student. Again here, the key is for the teacher to decide to what extent it makes sense to provide the instruction in the moment versus guiding the student toward other opportunities to learn. There is a fine balance between enabling students to depend too much on the teacher and frustrating students to the point of turning them off to learning. Teachers facilitate learning by providing just-in-time direct instruction.

Guide

Rather than provide instruction in the moment, the teacher might choose to guide a student to a resource for learning, such as a how-to sheet, podcast, website, textbook, or peer expert. A first-grade teacher meets with a small group of students. In the course of the conversation, a student needs a word that he can't recall. The teacher asks the group where he might find a word; another student in the group responds, "the word wall." As students look at the wall, the boy finds the word he wants. In this case, not only does the teacher resist offering up a word, but instead, guides the student to the word wall; the teacher doesn't divulge the word wall itself as the resource; the teacher asks students to identify the resource. In this case, the teacher's time is spent teaching resourcefulness more than content.

Guiding plays an important role in building executive function; and it is as important to teach executive function as it is to teach content. As learning facilitators, teachers should guide students in assessing their progress, setting goals, scheduling how to use their time, deciding what resources to use, etc. Teachers should guide students in recognizing their learning modality strengths and weaknesses, sometimes guiding students to challenge themselves to work outside their comfort zone. Teachers facilitate learning by providing students with guidance in making good decisions.

Encourage

Sometimes students don't need the answers or even guidance in finding the right learning resource; they simply need a little boost in confidence. Teachers can encourage students to persist in working through their current dilemma or questions. They can point to prior successes and assure the students that they have what it takes to succeed.

Encouragement is not a judgment of the student's worth or work; it is an affirmation that the teacher believes that the student can accomplish the task at hand. Words of encouragement focus less on work quality than on students' effort, tenacity, concentration, and other behaviors. Encouraging words include: "I have confidence in you; I know you can do this," "You always come through," "You've got what it takes," and so on. Encouragement should be aimed at helping the student stay with the learning struggle to reach success. Teachers facilitate learning by encouraging students to continue on their learning path toward achievement.

Celebrate

At times, facilitation will include celebrating success. This might be in the form of congratulating a student for arriving at a workable solution to a challenge, locating a powerful resource, mastering a particular skill, or other accomplishments related to academics or work habits.

Celebrating is not the same as praise. Simply put, celebrating is joining a student in the student's sense of accomplishment; praise is offering a judgment. Praise tends to attach a worth to an individual, with or without an accomplishment. Praise such as, "You're so smart," "You're so good," and "What a great book report," can be uplifting, but it can also work against students. Sometimes, the vagueness of praise can leave students misunderstanding what was valued. When teachers praise students by telling them that they're great, or that this was the best work the teacher has ever seen, they can set students up for future stress and failure to live up to that reputation. Teachers should avoid general praise in favor of specific feedback, such as, "Your opening statement is to the point; you use words that elicit emotion, which makes it very effective"; or "You and Tim stayed so focused for the past thirty minutes, and look what you accomplished!" The student then knows exactly what the teacher is thinking.

Celebrating is more about joining a student who recognizes an accomplishment and is proud. Using a variety of structures, such as rubrics, checklists, and goals, teachers can ensure that students know they have achieved success; and teachers can join their students in celebrating that success. Teachers facilitate learning by celebrating students' successes, motivating them to take on the next challenge.

Connect

Teachers who are facilitating connect students with other students, outside experts, and resources to assist them in their quest for learning. As teachers observe students engaging in learning activities, they can identify appropriate resources that would help students pursue their goals. The key is to avoid simply providing the answer in favor of connecting students to other resources through which the student will find the answer.

The teacher's advantage includes the whole-class and even multi-class perspective, engaging with all the students in the class and, in departmentalized situations, across classes. Teachers can suggest that one student talk with another who may have already encountered a similar situation. Teachers can create Peer Expert lists by asking students who demonstrate a high level of understanding of a skill or concept to add their names to the list; or teachers can create an online collaborative "Think Tank" where students post their "aha" moments; etc.

Depending on the level of technology in the classroom, teachers might connect students to outside experts and other students or teachers in the school through videoconferencing. Teachers might connect students to parent experts. Teachers facilitate learning by connecting students to others and to resources that will assist them in achieving their learning goals.

Question

Questioning is a key part of the facilitation process. Questions enable teachers to assess students' knowledge, foster cognitive progression, and probe student thinking. Teachers should ask students questions across five levels: comprehension, application, connection, synthesis, and metacognition.

Comprehension questions are those that assess students' basic understanding of the concepts, skills, and content that are the focus of the learning activity. If students are writing new ad campaigns for their favorite cereals, focusing on the use of adjectives, comprehension questions might include, "What is a noun?"; "What is an adjective?"; and "What is the purpose of an adjective?" If students are studying the New Deal in U.S. history, comprehension questions might include, "What was the economic state of the country when Franklin D. Roosevelt took office?" and "What was the Prohibition Amendment?" It's important for teachers to assess whether or not students possess a basic understanding of the content that will allow them to build higher levels of understanding and application. If students are using protractors to measure angles but do not possess the basic understanding of what an angle is and what an angle measurement is, they will only achieve at the level of procedural automaticity. Comprehension questions will determine if the student understands those concepts and, if not, allow the teacher to either connect the student to other resources or provide just-in-time instruction. The teacher might ask, "What is an angle?"; "What does the measurement of an angle represent?"; "What is an acute angle?"; "What is an obtuse angle?"; and "What is a right angle?"

Application questions are those that determine the extent to which students understand the content based on their ability to apply it to similar situations. As with the prior example, if students are learning to measure angles, a teacher might say, "Point out some acute, obtuse, and right angles you see in the classroom." Teachers might move students from paper to reality and ask them to measure some angles in the room. For students studying the Civil Rights Movement, a teacher might ask, "What groups today are in danger of having their civil rights restricted?"

Connection questions are those that determine the extent to which students can relate the content to their own lives. Retention of learning is enhanced when students can meld new information with existing schema (brain connections already in place to which new content can be linked).

For students studying the water cycle, a teacher might ask, "When have you experienced the water cycle in action?"; "Have you ever seen a glass with beads of water on the outside, or a window that steams up on one side?"; and "Have you ever seen a cloud? What do you think that is?" Students have most likely experienced rain and condensation. They may have experienced evaporation or make the connection that boiling water creates steam, the evidence of evaporation. Teachers should ensure that students make the connection between the content and their life experiences. For students studying poetry, the teacher might ask students to share a favorite poem or identify whether their favorite song lyric is in fact a poem. For students studying time signatures in music, the teacher might ask students to identify songs they like to determine the time signatures.

Synthesis questions are those that probe thinking and challenge students to engage in higher-order thinking, creating new knowledge from existing knowledge. An eighth-grade social studies teacher asked her students to review the U.S. Constitution to see if they would recommend any amendments. As I was visiting the class, two girls told me neither one of them could be President of the U.S. because they were not born in the U.S.; however, they moved here when they were very young. I asked if they were suggesting an amendment, and, as expected, they were crafting an amendment to allow naturalized citizens to become President. I asked if they felt anyone should be able to become a citizen and immediately run for President; they countered that the person would have to be a citizen for fourteen years. I then decided to present a more difficult situation and asked, "So if a two-year-old moves to the U.S., becomes a naturalized citizen, and then at the age of forty decides to run for President, you would be okay with that, yes?" They agreed. I continued, "And if a person who wishes to destroy the U.S. moves to the country at the age of twenty-five, becomes a citizen, waits fourteen years, and at thirty-nine, runs for President, you would be okay with that, yes?" That question was met with dead silence. They hadn't considered all angles. That led them back to the Constitution and their thought process to consider how they would widen their perspective. Synthesis questions often follow the thinking process of "So now what?" or "If you've accomplished this, what else could you do?"

Metacognitive questions are those that cause students to reflect upon their own thinking process. Teachers can ask students how they decided to tackle a problem, what path they took when they got stuck, how they arrived at their final answer, and so forth. They can also ask students how they liked working in particular ways and the difference between working as an individual versus a pair versus a group. Metacognitive questions fall into three categories: planning, monitoring, and evaluating (Tanner, 2012). Planning questions would include reflecting on the goals and the student's approach to achieving each goal. Monitoring questions would include reflecting on strategies that are or are not working, how the student can make the process and content more relevant, and considering factors that are slowing down the process. Evaluating questions would include how well the student accomplished the goals and what the student might do differently next time. Metacognitive questions support academic achievement as well as executive function.

Facilitation should not rely on the students' initiation of questions. When students are well engaged, it can be easy for teachers to simply check in to see if students need help; however, teachers must remember that students don't know what they don't know. Teachers facilitate learning by sitting next to students and asking them five levels of questions to both assess their learning and promote greater learning.

Glean

A key part of the facilitation process is gleaning information for formative assessment. As teachers observe, suggest, instruct, guide, encourage, celebrate, connect, and question, they gather critical assessment information that they can use to develop and assign future assignments and activities.

One of the advantages of a differentiated learning environment is that, with students working at their own cognitive levels, based on their personal learning preferences, the likelihood of academic achievement increases. One of the challenges of such a learning environment is ensuring that teachers are well aware of how each student is progressing so that they can facilitate each student's learning. An easy tool to use to glean formative assessment data is a facilitation grid (see Table 8.1).

A single unit of study may require multiple facilitation grids. For each grid, the teacher creates a list of concepts, skills, and content to be mastered across the top of the grid and the names of the students down the left side. While the grid becomes a linear checklist of content progression, it should not be used as such. Rather, it should be used as a repository for gathering observable data. Using the grid in Table 8.1, if during the course of facilitation, the student calculates the slope of a line using two points, the teacher might ask the student to explain how she arrived at that. If the student offers an accurate explanation, the teacher would place the letter "M" in that column under the student's row to indicate mastery. If the student explains the process well enough to teach another, the teacher would place the letter "P" indicating the student could serve as a peer tutor. If, on the other hand, a student is struggling to calculate the slope of a line, the teacher might place an "S" indicating the student should attend

Table 8.1 Facilitation Grid

Period 1	Plot a point given the coordinate pair	Identify the coordinate pair given a plotted point	Draw a line segment given two coordinate pairs	Draw a line given a linear equation	Explain "slope" of a line	Identify the slope of the line using the graph	Calculate the slope of the line using two points	Explain where one might use the slope of a line in real life
Sarah Abington								
Mike Arturo								
Leah Brooks								

M—mastery; **P**—peer tutor level; **HW**—needs homework for reinforcement; **W**—working on it; **S**—needs a small-group, mini lesson.

a small-group, mini lesson. Meanwhile, another student might be working on identifying the slope of a line using the graph with mixed success. The teacher would note that the student might need some homework by writing down "HW." The importance of the codes over simple checkmarks is that the codes provide a level of support needed, allowing the teacher to then design appropriate activities and assignments.

Teachers can use the facilitation grids to record formative assessment data gleaned during facilitation as well as to record test and quiz data. Looking horizontally across a row will indicate how a particular student is progressing, allowing the teacher to tailor assignments to build individual student achievement. Looking vertically down a column will indicate how the teacher's instructional plan is succeeding. If a number of students are struggling with a particular concept or skill, the teacher may need to rethink the learning activities and/or add a small-group, mini lesson. Teachers facilitate learning by gleaning formative assessment data and using it to make instructional decisions.

Design

During the facilitation process, teachers get to know their students as learners. This knowledge base helps them then design future instructional activities, employing the other insights from this book in the process. While standards should drive the *what* of instruction, teachers should design the *how*. Students may need more concrete experiences; some may need activities that focus on prerequisites not yet mastered; others may need extension activities to take their learning to a higher level; and so forth. Teachers can decide, upon looking at the facilitation grid and taking into account other information gleaned during facilitation, to offer small-group, mini lessons on skill instruction and whole-group benchmark lessons to introduce concepts students will soon need to achieve their goals. Teachers can decide what practice activities students need to reinforce learning and what learning activities they need to provide direct instruction on unknown or difficult content.

The Power of Facilitation

While it is easy to get lulled into thinking that busily engaged students want to be left alone, and they may even indicate so, it is important for teachers to remember that students don't know what they don't know. The facilitating teacher is a guide in the learning process, empowering students to find answers and solve problems, and providing them with inspiration and pathways. Through facilitation, teachers enact the philosophy of Socrates when he said, "Education is the kindling of a flame, not the filling of a vessel."

In Summary

Facilitating instruction to meet the demands of the CCSS requires:

- Designing a differentiated learning environment through which students engage in content

- Ensuring a mix of low-teacher-involvement and high-teacher-involvement activities

- Providing students with appropriate challenges to promote engagement in content

- Observing students, their thinking processes, and their work habits to make instructional decisions

- Suggesting ways in which students can progress in their thinking or skill development

- Providing direct instruction for those students who may be reaching a frustration point or who would do well to learn a concept or skill directly from the teacher

- Guiding students to others and to resources that will help them accomplish their goals

- Encouraging students to stick with a challenge

- Celebrating student success, both in academics and executive function

- Connecting students to others who may help in their pursuit of learning

- Asking questions to promote comprehension, application, connection, synthesis, and metacognition

- Gleaning formative assessment data to drive instruction

- Designing appropriate learning opportunities for students based on the formative assessment data gleaned

The *Learner–Active, Technology–Infused Classroom*

Courage is simply doing whatever is needed in pursuit of the vision.
—Peter Senge

The nonprofit organization What Kids Can Do, Inc. (www.whatkidscando. org) posted a YouTube video entitled *How Youth Learn: Ned's GR8 8*. The great eight video represents a compilation of ideas offered by students and is narrated by Ned, a teenager, offering eight conditions under which he learns:

1. **I feel okay**—Students' basic physical, psychological, emotional, and social needs are met so that they are not distracted.
2. **It matters**—The content relates to the real world or students' lives.
3. **It's active**—Students own the learning and engage with it.
4. **It stretches me**—Activities challenge the students' thinking.
5. **I have a coach**—Students have access to help and are guided in their learning activities.
6. **I have to use it**—Students solve problems, create new content, or teach others.
7. **I think back on it**—Students engage in metacognition regarding what and how they learned, and what they would have done differently in the process, learning from mistakes.
8. **I plan my next steps**—Students consider what to accomplish next, which causes them to transfer learning to new situations.

Ned's conditions for learning are reflected in the CCSS: Students must become active participants in a learning process that will provide both content mastery and the skills to learn throughout their lives; teachers must become the facilitators of their success.

The first chapter of this book offered a challenge to educators to develop students into problem-finders, innovators, and entrepreneurs by looking beyond the surface of the CCSS to embracing their very core. The last seven chapters offered some insights into making this happen (see Table 9.1). While

Table 9.1 The Seven Insights

Insight	Teachers' Actions
CCSS Achievement Requires Ends-Based Teaching	♦ Move beyond the "means" to engage student in "ends" activities
Understanding Requires Grappling	♦ Use problem-based learning to create a context for grappling ♦ Use "leveling up" to maintain momentum ♦ Ask probing questions that promote divergent and convergent thinking
Cognitive Progression Is a Lever for Achievement	♦ Break skills and concepts down into less complex understandings and build up to more complex understandings ♦ Minimize cognitive load in instructional activities ♦ Consider the progression of the CCSS across the years and attend to the necessary grade level understandings
The Power of Language Transcends the Disciplines	♦ Use literature to advance social and emotional growth toward academic achievement ♦ Teach three types of writing across the disciplines ♦ Focus students on communicating effectively with an appropriate audience ♦ View all subject areas as a descriptive language
Executive Function Is Foundational for All Learning	♦ Pair instruction in executive function with academic instruction to yield greater results ♦ Acknowledge that lack of executive function may have physiological roots and work to improve it
Purposeful Instruction Yields Retention	♦ Design instructional activities to address the three stages of learning: motivation, acquisition, and retention ♦ Develop learning activities and practice activities, each with their own purpose
CCSS Achievement Relies on Teacher Facilitation	♦ Use formative assessment to drive instruction ♦ Build high social capital through one-on-one and small-group engagement with students ♦ Use questioning to guide students' process and thinking ♦ Use a variety of participatory structures to promote achievement based on students' differentiated needs

each insight can be addressed by itself, designing a classroom that maximizes the interdependence of these insights will produce the greatest results. In this chapter, we'll explore such a classroom, as described in *Students Taking Charge: Inside the Learner-Active, Technology-Infused Classroom* (Sulla, 2011).

The *Learner-Active, Technology-Infused Classroom* is a student-centered learning environment in which students take charge of their own learning under the guidance of a masterful teacher. I use the metaphor of "teacher as ferry; teacher as bridge":

> Did you ever stop to consider the differences between taking a ferry or traveling a bridge to cross a river? Taking a ferry leaves the traveler in the hands of the boat operator and releases the traveler from all responsibility. The ferry operator tells you where to park your car, decides when the boat will leave and how fast it will move, and takes all of the travelers across at the same time and speed. Taking a bridge puts the traveler in control and in the seat of responsibility. Different drivers use different lanes and drive at different speeds. All who cross the start of the bridge at one time do not necessarily end up on the other side at the same time. The outcome is largely in the hands of the driver. But think about the magic of a bridge: a mass of steel suspended over a large expanse, being held in place almost miraculously, through the laws of physics. And yet probably few travelers hold that bridge in awe as they use it to move from one land mass to another, taking control of their travel, taking the bridge for granted.
>
> (Reprinted from the IDEportal,
> www.ideportal.com, with permission)

The teacher, as bridge builder, becomes the architect of a complex learning environment and the facilitator of learning as students take charge of their own learning. Some of the benefits are:

1. Building strong executive function and, thus, student responsibility for learning
2. Achieving high levels of student engagement
3. Pursuing high academic rigor

The role of the teacher shifts, along with how teachers use their time. In a conventional classroom, teachers spend time out of class grading and reviewing student work, with some time spent on planning lessons; in the *Learner-Active, Technology-Infused Classroom*, teachers spend most of their out-of-class time designing learning activities based on the use of formative assessment (and at first, problem-based units); they spend their in-class time assessing student work with the student(s) and guiding students in making wise instructional decisions.

This instructional approach employs a combination of the use of problem-based learning to drive academic content mastery, and a set of structures and strategies that support academic achievement and build executive function. With students deciding when to engage in what activities, the classroom can appear to be unstructured, depending on the student to drive the learning; in fact, it is the most structured classroom you'll find, depending on the teacher to guide students and provide the differentiated learning activities necessary for academic success. This chapter will walk you through the *Learner-Active, Technology-Infused Classroom* through the lens of the seven insights of making the CCSS work for you.

An Overview

The *Learner-Active, Technology-Infused Classroom* is the embodiment of these ten principles:

- ◆ High academic standards

- ◆ Learning from a felt need

- ◆ Student responsibility for learning

- ◆ Focusing on higher-order, open-ended problem solving

- ◆ Connected learning

- ◆ Individual learning path

- ◆ Working well collaboratively

- ◆ High social capital

- ◆ Technology infusion

- ◆ Global citizenship

When used in concert, these ten principles create a systems-based classroom that propels student achievement and aligns with the CCSS. The strength of the classroom, and thus its effectiveness, lies in the interdependence developed among these principles and the components.

At the core of the instructional approach is an Authentic Learning Unit (ALU), which consists of a problem-based task statement, an analytic rubric to drive instruction, a scaffold for learning offering differentiated learning and practice activities, and a facilitation grid through which the teacher gathers formative assessments. Supporting the ALU is a set of structures and strategies that build executive function, high social capital, and students' individual and collaborative learning skills. For example, students self-assess using a rubric and make decisions about what learning goals to pursue; they select appropriate activities and resources from a list provided by the teacher; they sign up for limited resources such as computers, specialized equipment, and learning centers. Teachers move about the room, spending two to five minutes per group or student to engage in deep conversations about the learning; they offer targeted small-group, mini lessons for direct instruction; they offer whole-class benchmark lessons to present concepts and trigger awareness of what students need to accomplish; and they gather formative assessment data they use in subsequent planning.

The Problem–Based Task

The first step to designing this learning environment is to chunk the curriculum into a four-to-six-week block of time (two to three weeks for primary-grade students). Teachers then decide what authentic, open-ended problems students could solve if they mastered all the content (see Table 9.2).

Table 9.2

Authentic	– A situation that could occur in real life – Fantasy is appropriate for primary and science fiction settings – If the situation is occurring in the students' lives, it is also "relevant," which is particularly important for high-school students
Open-Ended	– Having no one right answer – Non-Google-able – Teacher and student can assess effectiveness of solution using a set of criteria
Content-Focused	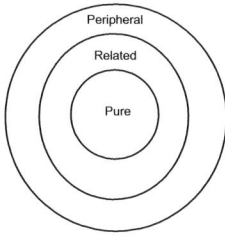
	– As much "pure" content as possible—the unit curricular objectives – Some "related" content is useful—particularly drawing on past and future subject-area objectives and CCSS-related ELA and math skills – Minimal "peripheral" content that is not related to the subject area

From the identified problems, students select an appropriate task intended to motivate and engage students. For example, students might plan and plant a vegetable garden using math and science skills; decide where the state might build a new airport; write to their favorite authors to convince the authors to write their next book about the students' town; devise an alternative fuel source; design the mathematical plan for an indoor ski slope; determine where to build a new resort to honor an ancient civilization; develop an effective immigration plan; paint an abstract representation of a social issue; and more.

Ultimately, students themselves should become the problem-finders and identify topics to pursue in the course of learning. As they research and develop solutions to those problems, they become innovators. As they simulate putting their ideas into action, they build the mindset of entrepreneurs. Some students, in fact, take their solutions beyond the classroom to the outside world, becoming social entrepreneurs.

While one problem-based task addresses a variety of standards, it is designed to keep the end goal of the standards in mind (chapter 2). The tasks typically focus on applying understanding, which creates a felt need for students to learn content. In the *Learner-Active, Technology-Infused Classroom*, the problem-based task is presented up front, before students have tackled any of the content. In the learning hourglass (Figure 7.1), it represents the motivation for learning. The task provides the students with a venue for grappling with content (chapter 3) and defines an end product the students will produce as they learn the unit content.

The Rubric

Next, teachers develop a rubric to provide students with clearly articulated expectations for the end product. In the *Learner-Active, Technology-Infused Classroom*, the rubric is meant to drive instruction, not assess learning. Given that students will be learning through the pursuit of the challenge presented in these problem-based tasks, and given that teachers will be facilitating instruction—providing direct instruction, guidance, and feedback throughout—the rubric would not be used to grade the end product but rather to allow students to self-assess and adjust their work accordingly. Grading the end product would be akin to grading the teacher, because it is the teacher's job to ensure that all students achieve success in designing the end product.

Toward that end, the rubric reads from left (novice) to right (apprentice, practitioner, and then expert) to offer a roadmap for success. The third column of the rubric, the *Practitioner* column, should read like a curriculum, laying out all of the skills, concepts, and content students are expected to master. It's appropriate for students to begin in the novice column and continually move toward greater achievement. The rubric is intended to be a vehicle through which students will self-assess and plan their learning activities. A well-designed rubric will lay out a cognitive progression across the row for students to continually build on their level of understanding (chapter 4). The rubric should be used to introduce academic and domain-specific vocabulary and model the use of deliberate and precise language to concisely convey meaning (chapter 5). As students use the rubric to self-assess and set planning goals, they build executive function (chapter 6).

Students should keep the rubric nearby at all times, referring to it to continually self-assess and set goals. As teachers facilitate, they should ask students to assess what they have accomplished and explain their plan for moving to the next level.

The Scaffold for Learning

Once the task and performance expectations are identified, the teacher then becomes the architect of a powerful learning environment to ensure student success. This begins with considering the various participatory structures through which students can learn, including:

♦ Whole-group "Benchmark Lessons" that last fifteen to twenty minutes and introduce key concepts across the course of the unit

♦ "How-To Sheets" offering students direct instruction through printed text to follow to accomplish a skill

♦ "How-To Videos/Podcasts" offering students direct instruction through a visual and auditory mix

♦ "Interactive Web Sites" allowing students to engage with on-screen manipulatives, participate in simulations, and explore concepts and skills

♦ "Small-Group, Mini-Lessons" that last ten to fifteen minutes, offered by the teacher to provide direct instruction in skills

♦ "Learning Centers" to engage students in hands-on learning experiences

♦ "Individual Tasks" aimed at building individual content mastery

♦ "Group Tasks" aimed at fostering divergent thinking, brainstorming, synthesis, and peer evaluation

- ◆ "Peer Tutoring" in which peer experts provide direct instruction in skills and concepts

- ◆ "Homework" through which students practice skills introduced and explored in class

- ◆ Other technology uses to build concepts and skills

It is through this brainstorming process that teachers identify rich and diverse opportunities for students to learn, allowing them to then design specific learning activities and practice activities. Teachers should take into account the best research-based best practices in instructional design when developing their Scaffold for Learning.

It is through the Scaffold for Learning that teachers design for purposeful instruction that yields retention (chapter 7) and consider how to leverage cognitive progression (chapter 4) to maximize student success. The scaffold is meant to help teachers think "outside the box" and brainstorm all of the ways in which a skill or concept could be addressed.

The Activity List and Schedule

From the Scaffold for Learning, teachers design instructional activities and corresponding activity lists that offer students: required activities that they must complete; choice activities that offer students multiple ways to address the same skill or concept, from which students choose one or more to complete; and optional activities that provide extensions based on interest and cognitive levels. Teachers design instructional activities that leverage cognitive progression (chapter 4) and employ purposeful instruction (chapter 7). Where possible, teachers design instructional activities that reflect the subject matter as a language (chapter 5), since language is a familiar component of our lives.

Students are responsible for making decisions based on the activity list and develop a schedule for how they will use their time over the course of a day or week, thus building executive function (chapter 6). Teachers help them in making these determinations, sometimes suggesting attendance at small-group, mini lessons.

Post-Design Teacher's Role

Once the ALU is designed and students are engaged in their pursuit of learning, the teacher's role shifts to that of learning facilitator, as detailed in chapter 8. The use of deliberate and precise language (chapter 5) provides important modeling during the facilitation process.

When students need help, they first refer to various structures, such as a quality work board, resource table, teacher's resource website, home group members, and peer experts. If they can't find the answer, they put their names on the help board, which the teacher uses during facilitation to determine which students to see next.

During class time, teachers engage in powerful content-related discussions with students on topics that arise during the course of facilitation. The learning environment is tailored to allow students to progress based on their own cognitive needs; thus, special-education students can learn alongside gifted students, all engaging in learning activities that are meaningful to them. Differentiation and diversity of experience abound.

The Co-Teaching Classroom

In most classrooms in which two teachers are assigned, three dominant instructional approaches take place: 1) the regular education teacher presents lessons while the special education teacher kneels down quietly beside a student, pointing to the place on a page or whispering helpful hints; 2) both teachers divide the class and teach to a smaller group; 3) one teacher provides lessons while the other grades papers. None of these are effective, nor do they make the special-education teacher, in particular, feel particularly efficacious.

The *Learner-Active, Technology-Infused Classroom* provides a venue for ensuring that multiple adults are used well in the course of the class period. With fewer whole-group lessons, both teachers can engage in facilitation as outlined in chapter 8, sharing the data gleaned and recorded on the facilitation grids with one another. Alternatively, one teacher can facilitate while one offers small-group, mini lessons or one-on-one conferences.

For schools looking to implement a Response to Intervention (RTI) initiative, the *Learner-Active, Technology-Infused Classroom* allows for all three tiers of instruction to take place in the same physical classroom. Essentially, students are engaged in solving compelling problems, relying upon the expertise of teachers to help them achieve, and utilizing the resources made available to them.

Standards-Based Instruction

The CCSS speak to a new world view of schooling, one in which students learn and retain learning, building upon it annually, to achieve at high levels of understanding and application; and one in which students build a combination of academic skills and executive function to tackle the challenges that lie ahead in college, career, and life. Change is never easy, but it is often worth the struggle. Those who work to pursue this new world view of schooling will reap the rewards of seeing resourceful, articulate learners emerge in front of their eyes. As systems theorist Peter Senge states, "Courage is simply doing whatever is needed in pursuit of the vision."

While much initial focus has been on *what* the standards say, the key to achieving the standards is *how* teachers think differently about instruction aimed at this level of achievement. Put to work in classrooms, the seven insights presented in this book begin to shift what instruction looks like. Combined with the *Learner-Active, Technology-Infused Classroom*, the seven insights create a powerful venue for standards-based instruction.

References

Carnevale, A. (2013). 21st century competencies for college and career readiness. *NCDA Career Developments, Spring*, 5–9.

Center on the Developing Child at Harvard University (2011). *Building the brain's "air traffic control" system: How early experiences shape the development of executive function: Working Paper No. 11.* Retrieved from www.developingchild.harvard.edu

Csikszentmilhalyi, M. (1990). *Flow: The psychology of optimal experience.* New York: Harper and Row.

Eliot, L. (2009, September 8). Girl brain, boy brain? *Scientific American.* Retrieved from http://www.scientificamerican.com/article/girl-brain-boy-brain/

Friedman, T. L. (2007). *The world is flat: A brief history of the twenty-first century.* New York: Picador.

Gattegno, C. (1987–2010). *What we owe our children: The subordination of teaching to learning.* New York: Educational Solutions Worldwide.

Getzels, J. W., & Csikszentmihalyi, M. (1976). *The creative vision: A longitudinal study of problem finding in art.* New York: Wiley.

Goin, M. (2009). *National Geographic readers: Storms!* Washington, DC: National Geographic Children's Books.

Hart Research Associates (2013). It takes more than a major: Employer priorities for college learning and student success. An online survey among employers conducted on behalf of the Association of American Colleges and Universities, Washington, DC. Retrieved from https://www.aacu.org/sites/default/files/files/LEAP/2013_EmployerSurvey.pdf

Jeremy. (2010, August 17). Re: What the pfc did for early humans [Web log post]. Retrieved from http://pfctyranny.com/tag/executive-function

Jonassen, D. H., & Land, S. M. (Eds.). (2012). *Theoretical foundations of learning environments* (2nd ed.). New York: Routledge.

Kolb, D. A. (1984). *Experiential learning experience as a source of learning and development.* Englewood Cliffs, NJ: Prentice Hall.

Lambert, C. (2012, July 24). Twilight of the lecture. *Harvard Magazine.*

Mar, R. A. (2011). The neural bases of social cognition and story comprehension. *Annual Review of Psychology, 62*, 103–134.

Miller, G. A. (1956). The magic number seven plus or minus two: Some limits on our capacity to process information. *Psychological Review, 63*(2), 81–97.

Miller, L. (2010, June 14). Fresh hell: What's behind the boom in dystopian fiction for young readers? *New Yorker*. Retrieved from http://www.newyorker.com/arts/critics/atlarge/2010/06/14/100614crat_atlarge_miller

Oatley, K. (2009, December 8). Changing our minds. *Greater Good: The Science of a Meaningful Life*. Retrieved from http://greatergood.berkeley.edu/article/item/chaning_our_minds

Paul, A.M. (2012, March 17). Your brain on fiction. *New York Times*, Sunday Review section, p. 6.

Perlroth, N. (2013, December 29). Solving problems for real world, using design. *New York Times*. Retrieved from http://www.nytimes.com/2013/12/30/technology/solving-problems-for-real-world-using-design.html?_r=0

Pink, D.H. (2012). *To sell is human: The surprising truth about moving others*. New York: Penguin.

Prensky, M. (2006). *Don't bother me mom—I'm learning*. St. Paul, MN: Paragon House.

Sawyer, R.K. (2006). *Explaining creativity: The science of human innovation*. New York: Oxford University Press.

Sousa, D.A. (2005). *How the brain learns*. Thousand Oaks, CA: Corwin Press.

Sulla, N. (2011). *Students taking charge: Inside the learner-active, technology-infused classroom*. New York: Routledge.

Sweller, J. (1988). Cognitive load during problem solving: Effects on learning. *Cognitive Science, 12*, 257–285.

Tanner, K.D. (2012). Promoting student metacognition. *CBE—Life Sciences Education, 11*, 113–120.

Tough, P. (2013). *How children succeed: Grit, curiosity, and the hidden power of character*. New York: Mariner Books.

Townsend, J.C. (2012, December 14). Educate for problem-solving, not factories. *Forbes*. Retrieved from http://www.forbes.com/sites/ashoka/2012/12/14/educate-for-problem-solving-not-factories/?&_suid=1398024193340066856239386342

Voskamp, A. (2011). *One thousand gifts: A dare to live fully right where you are* (19th ed.). Grand Rapids, MI: Zondervan.

Wagner, T. (2012). *Creating innovators: The making of young people who will change the world*. New York: Simon & Schuster.

Wittgenstein, L. (1958). *Philosophical investigations*. Oxford: Blackwell.

Workforce Now (2013). *Three major employers in SW Florida: Identification of critical position/skill gaps*. Fort Myers, FL: Regional Economic Research Institute. Retrieved from https://webadvisor.hodges.edu/aa_pdfs/WorkforceNow.pdf

World Economic Forum (2014). *Global risks 2014* (9th ed.). Geneva: Author.

Zhao, Y. (2012). *World class learners: Educating creative and entrepreneurial students*. Thousand Oaks, CA: Corwin.